Early Praise for Who Works Where [& Who Cares?]

This is one of the most practical how-to books to come along for leaders challenged with managing flexible work teams. The unique focus on TEAM and TRUST provides a strong framework for successfully implementing flexible work groups. It takes the mystery out of it!

- Karen Mathews, Director WorkLife Services, WellStar Health System

Flexwork technology has been available for over a decade. And employees who work remotely are more productive. So what's holding us back? Managers! If you have any plans to manage people or teams in the 21st century, buy this book. Dog ear its pages. Talk with your people. Join the movement of mobile managers who are kicking ass with high performing, highly connected teams, globally, 24-7-365.

- Rebecca Ryan, Futurist, Author, Next Generation Consulting

This book provides a toolkit that enables leaders at any level of an organization to ensure HOW their teams work together is the most efficient and effective way to accomplish their goals. It's a great resource for leaders who want to truly transform their workplace environment.

- Erika Chambers, Work-Life Director, University of Kentucky

Who Works Where may well go down as the ultimate guide book for organizations that want to do more than just talk the talk in workplace flexibility. It's a hands-on guide, rich with been-there-done-that tactics for maximizing the strategic value of flexible work.

- Kate Lister, President, Global Workplace Analytics

Who Works Where

[and Who Cares?]

A Manager's Guide to the New World of Work

Kyra Cavanaugh

Printed in the United States of America

First Printing, 2014

ISBN 978-0-991 4590-0-1

Life Meets Work Inc.
310 Busse Highway #310
Park Ridge, IL 60068

www.lifemeetswork.com

Table of Contents

Foreword   7

Preface   8

How to Use This Book   11

Introduction   15

Navigating Change   21

Team Goals & Metrics   27

Build Your Plan   37

Tool #1: Performance   57

Tool #2: Capacity & Resiliency   85

Tool #3: When & Where We Work   105

Tool #4: Work Process   119

Tool #5: Communication   129

Tool #6: Team Building   151

Keeping it Real   165

Templates   173

Acknowledgments   194

About the Author   195

To Joe, Nate, Sean & Tom,
you are the light of my world.

Foreword

It is no longer practical, nor does it make good business sense, to expect all employees to be physically present, in one place, at one time, to get their work done. There are exceptions, of course, due to the "role reality" associated with certain jobs. However, those with jobs that can be accomplished working somewhere other than the "mother ship" of an office should be allowed to do so, and the conversation around this has matured dramatically in recent years.

I will never forget the look in the eyes of the 100+ managers who sat staring back at our firm's CEO and me when we formally announced our "work anywhere, anytime" initiative over five years ago. There was a combination of excitement, disbelief, and fear. (That should have been our first clue that we had missed something.) Many of our managers had an engrained "If I can't see you, you're not working" paradigm, and our firm had countless draconian policies and processes in place to reinforce that belief. Suddenly they were gone.

It took us a while to realize there was one big hole. We had trained our managers on surface things (policies, procedures), but had given them little more than philosophical guidance about leading teams that are out of sight. Some adapted quickly and figured out intuitively how to adjust. Others did not.

Thankfully, we encountered Kyra Cavanaugh, President of Life Meets Work. She taught us how to fill the gap. As a result, we learned how to properly equip our managers with tools they need to lead successfully in this new world of work.

In her book, Who Works Where [and Who Cares?] Kyra provides a clear roadmap with solid guidance for those who are striving to ensure success in non-traditional work environments. The only criticism I have is that Kyra didn't write it years ago, before we began our journey!

> *- Delta Emerson, SPHR, Executive Vice President and Chief of Staff, Ryan LLC*

Preface

Ever since the rise of dual-earner couples, work-life experts have foretold the need for systemic changes in the workplace. Driven by a desire to prove that industrial-age workplace practices no longer fit the needs of the modern family, these forward thinkers built an impressive body of research.

But building the business case for change wasn't enough to overcome entrenched attitudes. After all, business leaders had built successful enterprises throughout the 20th Century using "un-family-friendly" work practices.

From Accommodating Individuals...

As some leaders became sensitive to the challenges of working parents, they implemented flexible work policies designed to help. In the beginning, becoming a "best workplace" meant sensitizing managers to the idea that some individuals needed "alternative" work options.

These accommodations were focused on the individual and gave them "permission" to ask for a flexible work arrangement. Flex was positioned as a benefit that could be taken away at any time, for any reason. As such, flexible work arrangements became an option for working parents who, out of courage and necessity, risked professional backlash to meet their work-life needs.

Truthfully, flexible work is still rooted in this approach. The pioneers of the work-life field did critically important work to raise awareness of the needs of the American family. And those organizations that led the charge by "doing the right thing" made a real difference in their employees' lives.

...To Workplace Change

But there's a problem with this legacy. Organizations check the box and say "okay we offer flexibility," when in reality what they have is "flex for anyone brave enough to ask." Today, even leading workplaces struggle to honor their commitment to workplace flexibility as many managers send the message that asking for flexible work is not really okay. And many employees don't ask because they're afraid of being seen as uncommitted or because they don't think their manager will support them.

To top it off, a number of new leaders in large companies in crisis, in very public declarations, have pulled back on flexible work policies. They plead the need for onsite collaboration and retrench to industrial-era work policies, erasing the gains made through individual accommodations.

But the solution to today's business challenges is not to go backwards and it isn't place-based either. The solution is to move forward as a team in a coordinated way—recognizing that change is required not because of the needs of a few, but because powerful trends are already reshaping the workplace. A number of forces are challenging our existing workplace structure:

- Technology
- Generational differences
- Globalization
- Baby Boomer retirement
- Overwork and stress
- Environmental sustainability

In the past, organizations could generally get away with ignoring the needs of the American family. But now it will be virtually impossible to be competitive without embracing fundamental changes to the workplace. Whether that change is manifested in workspace design, technology, or location, the modern manager will need tools to manage differently.

Not only will leaders need new skills to lead their teams, but organizations will have to let go of the notion that changes in *how*, *where* and *when* work gets done are the purview of the individual. Because now, making those changes will impact how effectively your organization competes and collaborates.

New Needs, New Skills

This book provides a simple framework that managers can use to organize their team around six aspects of what we call "team life." As you do so, you'll align the needs of individuals with the needs of the team, and ultimately the goals of the organization.

You'll create new rules of the road, designed specifically for your team, within the new definitions of workplace. And as a result, your team will deliver work more efficiently and effectively with fewer feelings of stress and overwork. Whether you're concerned about developing your own leadership skills for the new world of work, or you need to change your approach to meet the changes in your own workplace, this book will help you redesign the way you work.

How to Use This Book

If you're a middle manager, you're in a tough spot today. You're managing leadership pressure to do more with less and a workforce whose expectations are very different than the ones you grew up with. As a manager, you may be finding yourself in one of three camps: embracing change, resisting change, or hanging on for dear life somewhere in the middle.

Workplace change is coming in the form of internal mobility initiatives, open collaborative work environments, work from home initiatives, flexible work policies, and dispersed and globalized teams, to name a few. Managers, who feel challenged to manage the day-to-day workload of an onsite team can feel totally overwhelmed when considering how to manage a team of people working in all of these new ways.

So what's the solution?

In this book, we outline a straightforward tool that any leader, in any organization, can use to organize their team to work effectively in these new ways. Called a Team Alignment Plan, it provides a framework to initiate a conversation with your team around six aspects of "team life."

As you consider each of the components to working effectively together (as a global, flex, dispersed, distributed and/or virtual team), ask yourself: Which aspects of team life are we already doing really well? Which of these areas are we neglecting? And, once you've asked yourself these questions, ask your team what they think.

This book is written to spur thought and honest consideration about how your team can collaborate better and the ways in which your leadership style needs to change.

You'll find best practices, tips and advice culled from years of conversations and workshops with managers of varying degrees of experience in a variety of industries.

You'll be challenged by questions throughout the book to encourage you to think about how you can apply these best practices to your own team. Go ahead, grab a pen, and write your answers in the book.

Then draft a Team Alignment Plan for your team using the template on page 181. Engage team members to provide feedback and their own ideas before finalizing it.

Refer to it and regularly review it together so that it stays a relevant, guiding document for how you work together in the new world of work.

" The significant issues we face cannot be resolved at the same level of thinking we were at when we created them. **"**

- Albert Einstein

Introduction

The workplace is changing. There are signs of it everywhere—disappearing cubicle walls, brightly colored acoustic tiles, work at home policies, and tablets instead of laptops. Are you ready?

I don't mean *Are you ready to figure out how to have a private conversation with your co-workers sitting right next to you in your new open workspace?* I mean, *Are you prepared to lead your team through this change?*

Whether your workplace is embracing telework or is still clinging to corner offices for executives, it's time to hone the skills you'll need to successfully navigate the future of work.

Signs of Change

The obvious signs of change can be seen in technology and real estate. For instance, the average organization already has only seven desks for every 10 employees, and workspace will shrink 18% by 2020. In the U.S., organizations have an average of 3.45 network-connected devices per employee, but in places like Canada, Brazil, Australia, and India, the average is 5.4 or greater.[1]

What about the needs of the people you work with? How are they changing? Over half (54%) of working adults say they'd give up a percentage of their salary for more flexibility at work. Gen Y is more willing than any other generation to take a pay cut (an average of 14%) for workplace flexibility.[2] Another

---

1 Citrix Global Mobile Workstyles Index, 2012
2 Mom Corps Labor Day Survey, 2012

study found that 2 in 5 Gen Yers said they would take a lower salary in exchange for more flexibility in 'device choice, social media access, and mobility.'[3]   Note: Young professionals aren't the only ones driving change—72% of the 50+ workforce say they want flexible work schedules, too.[4]

Not only are the needs of each generation of employees different, but the cost of their stress and overwork on corporations is enormous. Analysts estimate that workplace stress costs U.S. employers hundreds of billions of dollars each year due to accidents, absenteeism, turnover, and medical costs.

Combine the speed of change in technology with the expectations of younger generations entering the workforce and it'll really make your head spin. Anyone who currently has an elementary school-aged child knows that the workplace of the future is going to have to look completely different than it does today.

We're Too Busy

What about the not-so-obvious signs of change? Think about disengagement in the workforce, the blurring of the workday in this 24/7/365 world of connectivity, diminished investment in learning and development, and individual isolation and organizational disconnection. In this intensely stressful world of work, we're investing less time in people. We're simply too busy.

The impact of all of this change on individuals is hard enough. But what about the impact on your team? Do they recognize the need for change, or have they been clamoring for it all along? Are you innovating your work processes? Letting go of low value work? Are you enabling team members to work from home?

What about collaboration and trust? Do you and your team members trust each other? Are you collaborating effectively?

Or, are you so busy with the day-to-day, tactical aspects of your business that you

3 Cisco 2011 Connected World Technology Report
4 Staying Ahead of the Curve 2013: AARP Multicultural Work and Career Study

haven't lifted your head to look around and see that your team is no longer performing optimally?

It Used to be Different

You might ask yourself, "What business is it of mine anyway?" Especially if you work in an organization that isn't innovating their workplace practices, it's easy to ignore the change that's happening around you. "No time for strategy right now. No reason to think differently about how my team operates. I just have to make it through another day," you tell yourself. Until you, yourself, grind to a halt. Until you hear that voice in your head telling you it used to be different. You used to take a lunch…with co-workers…at a restaurant. You used to laugh, work used to be fun—or at least more fun than it is today.

The future of work will have to be different. You will need to be an advocate both for individuals on your team and for process innovations that will help you all deliver better results. You'll need courage to engage your team and advocate for change. You'll need to break the rules and create new ones, leading the way so that your peers will follow.

You'll need to step away from outdated modes of thinking about the workplace. You'll have to build trust without the benefit of face time. And you'll need to collaborate using technologies that feel sub-optimal at times.

Adapting to workplace change is a challenge—a challenge best faced with optimism and an open mind. Be willing to step outside the day-to-day craziness of your job to adopt new skills and plan for the future. Invest time and attention in things you may not think matter right now and be committed to a future that's bigger than yourself.

In this book, you'll learn a simple, straightforward approach to lead your team through this changing landscape. Through this process, you'll have the opportunity to improve efficiency, client service, productivity, employee engagement, collaboration and more.

The Importance of Trust

In our workshops, I tell participants that we're going to start by talking about big, theoretical constructs and then bring them down to practical reality as quickly as possible. Words like trust, collaboration, integrity, values—people throw those words around a lot. But what do leaders who use these words really mean? Trust is one of those concepts that can be defined in a hundred different ways and can feel very heady to try to understand.

Yet, trust is at the center of effective and meaningful relationships—something most of us crave in our work. As managers of teams who aren't all working in the same place anymore (at least not all the time), the challenge is how to build trust. In a recent workshop, I overheard a manager say, "I never trust anyone I work with who isn't in the office with me." When asked why, he said, "I've never felt comfortable building a relationship with someone I can't see. I have no idea who they are or what they're doing."

I appreciated his honesty, but those attitudes are simply not feasible in the world of work today. Many managers wonder:

- How can I build trust when I can't read your non-verbals or when we haven't had the benefit of working in the same office for years?

- How can we form positive "I've got your back" relationships when we come from different cultures, struggle through regional accents, or have different expectations about what it means to show up for work?

This poses a major challenge, especially for managers for whom face time was a key component of building trust in the past (or even in the present).

In our workshops, we do an exercise in which we ask managers to identify specific behaviors that build trust and behaviors that erode it. Then we ask them to study the lists and be honest with themselves about how many of those behaviors they exhibit.

It might be eye-opening to realize that being perpetually late for a meeting is eroding a team member's trust. Or you might be surprised that simply saying good morning regularly, even via IM, builds trust.

Have open conversations with your team about trust. Talk about behaviors that build and erode trust. Discuss ways to increase (or decrease) those behaviors to improve trust among team members—across time zones, countries or flexible work arrangements.

Ask your team members whether they start out trusting others and then lose trust over time, or whether they need to build trust over time. Where are you on that spectrum? Share your own approach to trust with your team.

Without trust, team performance breaks down. But building trust doesn't necessitate being in the same work location. Building trust is about recognizing that everyone's expectations are different. Talking about those expectations is a good first step.

Collaboration is Misunderstood

What is collaboration and why is it seemingly in such short supply in the modern organization? Organizations today are on a mission to get people to collaborate more. It's as if collaborating (or cooperating or communicating) is the end goal.

Collaboration, by definition, is about HOW teams of people work together to reach a common goal. So let's break this down. Companies who want to improve collaboration want to do so to achieve a goal. What goal? Better productivity, more innovation, better customer service?

When your company says, let's implement an open plan for our workspace, or let's tell all of our employees they can't work from home anymore because we need to COLLABORATE better, the first question you need to ask is why? What are we trying to accomplish by collaborating better?

If we can be honest about the goal we're using collaborative work practices to

Despite what many business leaders think today, there is more than one way to collaborate. Thanks to technology, we don't all have to be in the same place at the same time. Instead, we need to be innovative and take risks to learn how to use technology in new and different ways.

achieve, then we can get creative about how we collaborate.

The goal comes first. The path to reach that goal is open to redefinition.

Now the fun begins because there are lots of tools you can use, in infinite combinations, to reach your goal. In this book, we suggest six of them. And the beauty is that these six tools can help you improve collaboration (to reach your goal) in a way that can be as customized and specific as your work function, industry, and workspace definition.

Better yet, we'll show you how to engage your employees to build this collaboration plan together to meet the needs of each individual team member while still meeting your functional and organizational goals. Since everyone on the team participates in developing the plan to improve collaboration, you build stronger bonds of trust and performance improves.

Using this process, you can avoid narrowly defining WHERE that work takes place. With the goal in mind, the tools in place and the practices defined, it doesn't matter whether people are working onsite, at home, in a coffee shop, or from a satellite office. It doesn't matter because everyone is clear on HOW the work will get done and is held to their performance goals.

The end result: Leaders can accomplish their goals, improve collaboration and let go of being so invested in bringing everyone back into the office.

Navigating Change

"I've been trying to make this flex work model work for me, and the biggest challenge I'm finding is that I have the burden to make it work—companies are only willing to allow it if I don't make it at all "inconvenient" for them. It's not really a flexible schedule in many ways. What will it take to make this really change??

- Attorney, pharmaceutical company

Navigating Change

Building a Team Alignment Plan is really about managing change. So let's start by identifying the change facing your team and the challenges that it brings.

Think about how your team currently operates and think about what you would like to change. Change can feel exciting or challenging. Either way it brings you, as a manager, the opportunity to encourage new behaviors and new attitudes with your team members.

What changes are you facing and what challenges would you like to address?

Common challenges facing teams today:

- **Flex Work & Telework:** Many teams are undergoing a major shift in the way they work. Perhaps your organization has implemented a workplace flexibility initiative that enables people to work fewer, longer days. Or, they can shift when they start or stop their workday. Perhaps more and more people are working from home.

- **Globalization:** Teams are dispersing across the country and even the world. Perhaps you have team members working in multiple locations. Differences in culture, language, work styles or personalities can all play a role in changing the ways you need to lead.

- **Open Plan Workspaces:** Some organizations are tearing down the cubicle walls. Teams are being encouraged to collaborate in café environments... sitting at a farm table...on exercise balls...alongside the CEO.

- **Resiliency:** Years of stress and doing less with more have taken their toll on the workforce. You may be losing team members or simply noticing people have become disengaged.

Once you identify the challenge you want your team to overcome, then you'll be able to determine what the future looks like.

For each one of us, the future of work looks different.

List the challenges your team is dealing with that are prompting you to look for a new way to work together:

_____

_____

_____

_____

_____

What's Your Challenge?

- ☐ Acclimating to an open floor plan
- ☐ Working better with your offshore team
- ☐ Better managing a team located across the U.S.
- ☐ Retaining your young professionals
- ☐ Retaining boomer knowledge
- ☐ Managing a multi-generational team
- ☐ Managing a flexible work team
- ☐ Managing people who work from home

What would you like your team to be able to do better, or to accomplish together? What would you like to change?

_____

_____

_____

_____

_____

What will the future of work look like for you and your team? Think not only about where your team members will be working and what devices they'll be using, but also HOW they will work together.

_____

_____

_____

_____

_____

We've developed this set of principles that everyone on our team agrees to follow, so that we can improve team mobility while maintaining our strong company culture.

Turn to page 181 to capture the change happening in your workplace.

One Manager's Decision

A manager at a manufacturing company honored a couple of employees' requests for flexible work arrangements, but didn't want to give the option to everyone on his team. He worried that if he made flex options available to everyone, they'd all want to work from home and no one would be left in the office to answer the phones.

But this manager was challenged by his organization to do more. So when he started developing his Team Alignment Plan, he decided his goal was to build a fully flexible work team where employees could flex their schedules as they needed, working together to consider the needs of the business.

Team Goals & Metrics

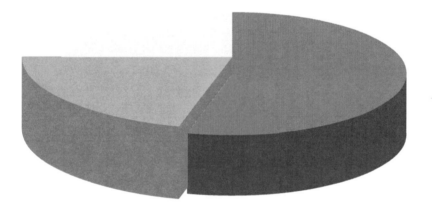

" Through the process we found some things that we didn't realize made us really good at who we were and what we do. It helped us be better communicators and a better functioning group overall. "

- Manager, professional services firm

Team Goals & Metrics

In most organizations, goal setting flows from organization to individual, without stopping to focus on team goals. Managers, who are responsible for department level functions, have their own goals and, of course, are charged with overseeing individual goals. But who's looking after the team?

Setting team goals reinforces to team members that their contribution to the team is part of what you value about their work—it's not just about getting their own work done. Survey after survey shows that employees want to know that their work matters, that they matter. They want confirmation that they are contributing to something bigger than themselves. Especially in large organizations, it may be more realistic to see one's impact on their team than on the organization as a whole.

When you set a team goal, it gives everyone something to rally around—it gives work more meaning, provides context and improves engagement. It helps team members feel useful and connected, like you're facing the future together.

Team Goals Can Be Simple

An extroverted manager of a small team of introverts wanted to improve team interaction. She believed that if she could only figure out how to connect with them in the right way, they would share their ideas with her and they could serve their clients better. She'd tried everything—bringing donuts to work, taking them to lunch and nothing worked. She wanted to try new team building skills for introverts as part of her plan. She knew she had achieved her goal when they started regularly sharing their ideas with her. She used the volume and quality of team member ideas as her metric to know she was making progress.

So what kind of goals do teams set? Some prefer a quantitative goal like improving delivery time or safety. Others prefer qualitative goals like having more fun, or feeling more connected.

Here are some examples of team goals that other managers have set:

- Improve collaboration
- Improve quality
- Improve delivery time
- Innovate new work processes
- Make time for fun
- Improve employee engagement
- Increase the visibility of your team
- Eliminate low value work
- Improve time management
- Make meetings more efficient
- Increase safety
- Reduce turnover or absenteeism
- Improve customer service or net promoter scores
- Try new technology

The Team Alignment Plan encourages managers to be entrepreneurs of their own teams. It strengthens the bonds between team members and manager, creating a snowball effect. When enough teams do this work, the culture of the organization itself starts to change.

Can you think of something you'd really like your team to do better? Something you've talked about in the past, or that you believe is important now?

_____

_____

_____

What are some team goals you'd like to consider to benchmark your change effort?

_____

_____

_____

_____

Our professional commitment as a team is to our clients and delivering high quality engagement results, while adhering to our company's policies and procedures. Our goal is to accomplish this high level of client service by juggling our professional responsibilities with our personal needs throughout each day, week, or month.

The goal of this agreement is to identify the values and actions that each of us should exhibit as a member of this team.

SAMPLE: TEAM GOAL

Turn to page 181 to draft your team goal(s).

There's no point in setting a goal, if you don't know whether you achieved it.

I was speaking with the head of real estate of a large research company. His goal was to reduce the company's real estate footprint and transition 1,000 employees to work from home on a permanent basis. He told me about the millions of dollars this move would save the company.

"But how will you know when you are successful?" I asked.
"What do you mean, we're going to save millions of dollars!"
"Beyond initial real estate savings, how will you know the initiative was a success?
"Well, I never thought of that."

If this company saved on real estate costs, but suffered service declines, would the move be considered a success? And on the flip side, if a new CEO came in three years after the transition and wanted to move everyone back into the office, but was told that product delivery times had improved by 20%, would s/he still be so tempted to reverse course?

When you think about the challenges facing your team, how will you know that you've succeeded? There are lots of metrics that you can use to judge success, and sometimes those measures can even be qualitative, not quantitative. No matter what kind of metric you use, you should have a way of determining whether the changes were beneficial.

Identifying Your Metric

Leading your team to work in new ways is an opportunity not just to embrace change, but to celebrate it. When you think about successfully managing your team through change, how will you know that you're getting it right?

_____

_____

_____

Will you be able to quantitatively measure the change (perhaps with increases in customer service scores or employee turnover declines)?

_____

_____

_____

_____

Or will the change be more qualitative (team members will take more risks, or laugh more, or more enthusiastically provide feedback or solve problems more proactively)?

_____

_____

_____

_____

When you and your team have successfully navigated change, how will you all act or behave differently? What will be measurably different about your performance?

_____

_____

_____

_____

We're going to measure our effectiveness as a team through these metrics:

1. Higher productivity
2. Better engagement
3. Faster response time
4. Greater project knowledge
5. Increased confidence and comfort in leading meetings

Turn to page 181 to draft your ideas for the metrics you'll use to measure your team goals.

Talk to Your Team

Once you've determined your metrics, communicate your vision and goals to your team. Talk to them about the change facing you and the opportunity it presents. Engage your team members at the beginning of the process to get their buy-in and build transparency around your effort. You're all going to need to work together, sharing ideas and investing time in solutions. Start by including them now.

A Word About Teams

How do you define a team? We get this question all of the time in our workshops. For the purposes of developing a Team Alignment Plan, your team can be:

- Your direct reports

- Your entire department or organization within which there are multiple sub-teams

- Your entire organization

- A project team or matrixed team made up of people who will work together until a particular goal is accomplished

The most important consideration is: with whom do you need to agree on how you will operate together?

We've seen a department head work with his directors to develop the framework of "non-negotiables" for everyone in his department and then ask his managers to customize from there for each of their teams of direct reports.

We've seen leaders work with their entire organization of 25 people to determine their plan together, even though there were managers with smaller teams that could have formed their own.

And plans have been developed by project teams where the team members change but the leader stays the same. That leader works with the initial project team to develop the plan, and then renegotiates it with each new project team she's responsible for.

Build Your Plan

“ I'm familiar with a lot of tools for team action planning, but this is far more comprehensive than anything I've seen. **”**

- Director, food manufacturer

Build Your Plan

Picture yourself and your team preparing to go on a camping trip in the woods of northern Minnesota for a week. Everything you'll need must be carried in on your back. There will be no running water, electricity or even cell phone coverage. How will you prepare for your trip?

You organize a meeting with everyone to agree on the goals of the trip and get a plan together for everything that needs to be accomplished. Settling in with a cup of coffee, Pete says he's hoping for a week of solitude and quiet. Sara says she's ready for an adventure and wants to push herself every day of the trip. Ally is an amateur photographer who wants some really great scenery, especially a shot of a moose in a lake.

At this point you wonder whether you'll be able to get everyone on the same page. But before you tackle the big objectives, you decide to start with something simpler: the packing list.

Pete and Ally weigh in on the things they think will be most critical to pack, but you disagree with some of their choices. They've never done this, nor have you, so how do you really know what is important or optional, or even how you're going to fit everything in your pack?

This is getting overwhelming. Sara suggests that it might be easier to know what to pack if you decide your route. How many miles will you hike every day? How much down time will you plan for? What is realistic given the weight of your packs?

That leads to a whole other set of questions. How much weight can the average person carry? Is the group fit enough to handle this? Do we have all of the equipment we need? What is the budget for this trip anyway?

Faced with all of these decisions, and knowing there are plenty more you haven't even discussed, you have a choice to:

A. **Wing it.** Too many choices means too much complexity. As the leader of the group, you're going to pick a route, tell everyone to bring what they think they need, and go.

B. **Plan it.** Faced with all of these details, you talk with some experts, discuss options with your group and make a plan.

It might sound like a bad idea to wing it when faced with a big trip and no cell phone coverage! But that's exactly what leaders (and teams) do at work, all the time. Faced with a lot of opinions and uncertainty, a lack of resources, too little time and too much work, it's hard to stop and organize everyone. It's hard to find time to determine your choices or even feel like you have any.

So the suggestion that you stop and plan how you'll work together as a team can feel overwhelming and unnecessary. Or, it can feel like the solution to a set of problems you haven't been able to overcome until now. Here's what I mean...

Change of any kind, like changes to how, where and when people work, can serve as a catalyst for shoring up those less than efficient work practices that need attention. Now you have an excuse to reign in the employee who perpetually shows up late for a meeting or doesn't prepare in advance. You have a reason to stop and clarify expectations about the values and the behaviors you expect team members to exhibit when they work for you.

Rather than new ways of working being an impediment to collaboration, they become a catalyst for collaboration.

Clarify your expectations and work with your team to build a plan for how you will work together better, in more efficient, effective and fun ways. Collaboration will improve, trust will improve and performance will follow.

Plan ahead, and you won't get caught in the woods without sufficient food or water.

10 Elements of a Team Alignment Plan

1. **Navigating Change**
   Why are you embarking on this change?

2. **Team Goal**
   What are you trying to change as a team?

3. **Team Metrics**
   How will you measure success toward your team goal?

4. **Tool - Performance**
   What practices will you put in place to ensure that everyone is making progress toward their individual goals?

5. **Tool - Capacity & Resiliency**
   How do you divide up work to optimize your resources? How do you ensure that individuals stay resilient and engaged?

6. **Tool - When & Where We Work**
   Where and when can team members work in order to honor their own needs and the needs of the team? What are the expectations about when/where to collaborate vs. individual work time?

7. **Tool - Work Process**
   Have you established work processes that maximize collaboration and innovation, reduce low value work and support team members working anywhere?

8. **Tool - Communication**
   How will you enable open, honest and timely communication using varying forms of technology to stay connected and performing optimally?

9. **Tool - Team Building**
   Do you invest time to build a trusting, fun and resilient team? How will you maintain connection every day, throughout the year, anywhere team members are working?

10. **Keeping it Real**
    How will you keep this Team Alignment Plan alive? How often will you review it as a team? Who will take the initiative to keep it top of mind?

You'll find a sample Team Alignment Plan at the back of this book. There, you'll see how one team defined the sections Navigating Change, Team Goals and Team Metrics (which we already covered in earlier chapters). This sample also includes the six tools that follow. For a free, online version of the template you can use to complete your own, please visit www.lifemeetswork.com.

How to Eat an Elephant

Do you really need a plan? You may think you don't need to build a plan because you already talk with your team about:

- Day-to-day tactical issues
- Performance breakdowns
- Personal issues
- Project risks

But are you regularly discussing:

- Ways to eliminate redundant or low-value work?
- How to prioritize workload so employees don't burn out?
- The flexibility needs of your team members?
- Who is burning out in their role?
- The health and resiliency of your team overall?
- Your own expectations and aspirations for your team?

You may not think you need to discuss these things because your team members will come to you if they have an issue. No news is good news, you don't need to TALK about everything, you're already functioning fine, and there's no time.

There's a problem with this way of thinking.

If you don't stop to have the important conversations while trying to sell more, deliver more, achieve more, attain more and get the job done, you fail to lay the groundwork for a productive team.

Every manager dreams of a team that is efficient, resilient, reliable, innovative and committed to moving your business forward. But that team doesn't drop out of the sky. You have to work at it. You're responsible for building your dream team...but not to the detriment of the individuals you work with.

What's the Solution?

Building a Team Alignment Plan creates opportunities to have conversations with your team members that align your goals with their aspirations. Your plan will help your team perform better AND help you get comfortable with the idea of team members working in new ways that help them (and you) be more effective at work and at home.

You know the old adage, one bite at a time. The goal is to build a plan. But the approach you take is up to you:

- Some managers draft a plan, share it with their team to get feedback and make revisions before finalizing their plan.

- Others ask their team to divide into sub-groups and each take a section of the plan. Once drafted, the manager compiles the sections, makes revisions and shares the draft for feedback before finalizing it.

- Managers who have just one or two direct reports often use the plan as a discussion guide for a series of meetings over a period of time. The team reaches agreement on their work practices verbally. Sometimes they formalize the discussions in writing, and sometimes they leave the plan undocumented, knowing they've reached agreement on how to proceed.

One company took documenting these plans one step further. Managers there post their plans to a file on a shared drive that anyone in the organization can access. This level of transparency makes it easier for employees to determine whether they'd like to join a manager's team. Plus, it creates healthy competition when managers can see how other leaders are running their teams. It also enables best practice sharing when teams can compare their plans.

Benefits of Documenting Your Team Alignment Plan

- It gives you, as a leader, an opportunity to convey what is important to you and enables team members to push back and negotiate with you in areas that don't feel realistic or feasible for them.

- It reduces guesswork and productivity losses due to misunderstandings.

- New team members can get up-to-speed quickly.

- This document becomes a reference point for expectation setting with team members if they aren't exhibiting the behaviors you agreed on.

- It feels official. It's much harder to "break the rules" when they've been written down and everyone has agreed to follow them.

The Difference Between Planning and Micro-Managing

Does the Team Alignment Plan sound like micro-managing to you? The general consensus among the managers we train is that getting to this level of detail would only be micro-managing if you came up with the plan and told your team members that this is how it's going to be. Since this approach involves working with your team to build a plan together, everyone has input that prevents it from feeling stifling.

In the National Workplace Flexibility Study, employees felt even more supported by their managers after completing a team plan. By working together as a team to honor and recognize individual capacity and work-life needs AND business needs, managers and employees felt better, not worse.

After completing a Team Alignment Plan, 55% of managers indicated that team communication improved, 41% reported team understanding of performance goals improved, 24% said customer service improved, and 20% said productivity improved.

Which of the three approaches on page 43 would you like to use to build your plan?

_____

_____

_____

_____

However you decide to do it, after your plan is finalized, determine how frequently you'll review your plan as a team and make adjustments: monthly, quarterly, or annually. Also determine the forum for revisions: as part of a monthly team meeting, as its own standing quarterly meeting, as part of an annual retreat day, etc.

How often will you and your team review the plan?

_____

_____

_____

In what setting?

_____

_____

_____

It might help to think about building a Team Alignment Plan as a journey. You know where you are now, and you have a vision for what the future of work looks like in your organization. In order to get there, consider the six tools you and your team will need to effectively work together: Performance, Capacity & Resiliency, When & Where We Work, Work Process, Communication and Team Building.

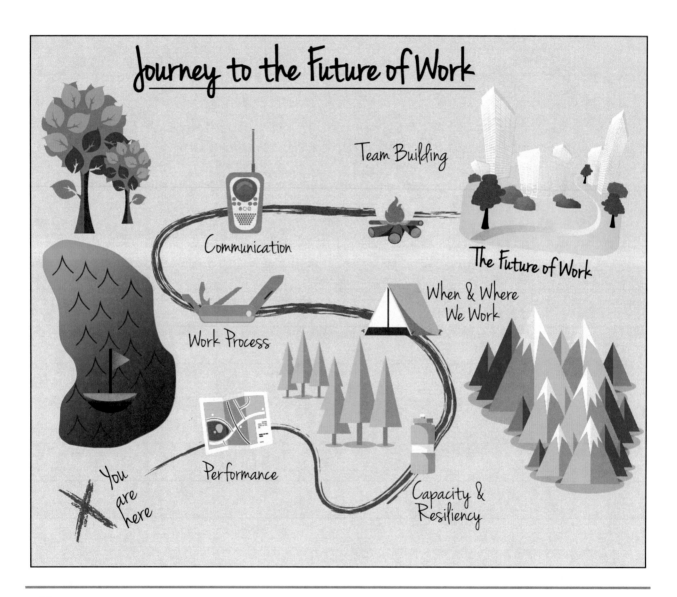

Why six tools? *Where did they come from?*

We've spent years training managers on how to build effective teams that are prepared to work in new and innovative ways.

In 2011, we embarked on a study with Career/Life Alliance Services and Boston College Center for Work and Family to study the impact of this approach on flexible work teams at MedImmune, Ryan LLC, and Minnesota Department of Transportation. At each of these organizations, managers were charged with leading teams of people in which some worked from home, worked condensed work weeks or worked flexible schedules. Still others managed geographically dispersed teams.

Some managers felt like they were already quite skilled at managing dispersed and/or flexible work teams, while others resisted the change toward working in these new ways.

We conducted workshops with these managers to train them on a team-based approach to establishing an effective, distributed work team. We surveyed the managers and their team members before and after the workshops, and we conducted a range of post-training activities that included conference calls and webinars to reinforce best practices and help managers build their action plan.

The results of this study showed that when managers worked with their teams to figure out how they were all going to work effectively in these new ways, employees felt better supported, engagement improved, and managers felt more comfortable with these new ways of working. They felt that customer service and productivity improved, and they became less concerned that these new ways of working would add to their workload.

With the rise of open, collaborative workspaces, we noticed that teams (and individuals on them) were stressed by different factors (including loss of privacy, noise/distractions/interruptions, workspace choice, me vs. we space, etc.) that needed to be worked out.

Similar to teams working flexibly or remotely, these teams also needed to negotiate expectations and boundaries around how they work together and how they would collaborate. They needed guidance on how to work as a team when the new workspace challenged employees' privacy, workstyle preferences, and sense of identity. Our planning approach gave teams an opportunity to redesign work process, clarify expectations, and work together to stay connected and redefine collaboration.

Lastly, we noticed an increase in resiliency for teams that had gone through the process. The University of Minnesota is researching the impact of this process on stress and health outcomes and is expected to publish its results late in 2014.

We encourage you to work with your team to agree on how you'll use these tools to reach your destination together—in sync—optimizing everyone's skills, innovating for efficiency, checking your packs, and supporting each other along the way.

Which tools do you think you and your team have already clearly defined?

_____

_____

_____

How do you know?

_____

_____

_____

Which tools do you need to better define?

_____

_____

_____

Why?

_____

_____

_____

Which of these do you want to focus on? Rank them in order of importance to you, then ask your team to rank importance to them. Combine this feedback with the results of your self-assessment (found at the end of this chapter) to help you focus in on the areas that matter most.

_____

_____

_____

_____

The Devil is in the Details

In our workshops, we ask managers to gather in fictional teams and try to draft a plan, on the spot, for how they would work together in whatever new work structure is facing them. It could be that they're all moving to a new floor with lots of "WE" space and smaller "ME" space, or it could be their members are going to be dispersed all over the country. In 20 minutes, they need to build a plan for how they are going to work together to win the fictional "most collaborative team" award in their organization.

> ### WE vs. ME Space
>
> ME space = individual assigned space
>
> WE space = shared space
>
> Increasing the proportion of WE space to ME space in workplace design encourages internal mobility. Employees move about throughout the day, picking spaces that reflect the type of work they're doing at any given time. This shift is supported by mobile technology, wireless internet, and a desire to encourage employee freedom of choice in where and how they work.

Some teams focus their full 20 minutes on negotiating when they're available for meetings and what technology they'll use to communicate. Others create friendly competitions to build transparency around which team members are the most productive. By and large though, everyone struggles with the details. Creating a laundry list of everything that needs to be decided can be overwhelming, just like the camping example at the beginning of this chapter.

These managers recognize the need to be more specific, but they don't know how to get there.

As I review their plans, the conversation goes something like this.

Me: "How are you going to communicate with each other when you're not all working in the same location?"

Them: "We're going to have one-on-one meetings, and use email, IM and phone calls when we need to reach each other."

Me: "What does that really mean? Who is going to initiate the request? Who is calling whom? Is it a standing meeting at a set time? How frequently? For what duration? Who is running the meeting? What types of topics are appropriate? Is there a format to follow? Is it mandatory that everyone attend?"

"And how are you going to track project status? Are you sending weekly status updates or waiting for a meeting? If you're sending weekly updates, do you send them to everyone or just your boss?"

"Your plan needs to be specific. And if you're not sure you're being specific enough, ask yourself this question: If I joined your team on Monday, would I know how you operate? Or would I spend my first three months reading the tea leaves to try to figure it out?"

Them: "Okay, we get it. We're being too general. There's a lot to consider."

The rest of this book is designed to help you work through those details. We'll take you through each of the tools, providing food for thought, ideas and suggestions based on the experiences and best practices of others. This will help you guide your team to be as specific as possible in your plan.

Readiness Assessment

To help you decide which tools you and your team need to develop the most, take this self-assessment. Read through the questions and circle your answer: yes (Y), maybe/sometimes (S) or no (N).

Measuring Results

I find it easy to hold my team members accountable.	Y	S	N
I meet with team members at least once a month to provide feedback and discuss their progress towards goals.	Y	S	N
We have one clear metric that we measure success by on our team.	Y	S	N
I work with each of my team members to set measureable goals.	Y	S	N

Performance

The behaviors I see from my team members align with my expectations for what success looks like on my team.	Y	S	N
I have a vision for team success and everyone on my team understands and agrees with it.	Y	S	N
My team members understand how their roles contribute to the success of the team.	Y	S	N
We are good at holding each other accountable for individual performance.	Y	S	N

Capacity & Resiliency

I feel confident piecing together the puzzle of everyone's capacity each week.	Y	S	N

Team members regularly pitch in to help if someone has too much work on their plate.	Y	S	N
I know which of my team members have too much (or not enough) work to do.	Y	S	N
We regularly meet as a team to discuss progress, workloads and barriers to accomplishing our goals.	Y	S	N
I feel I am supportive of my team members both personally and professionally.	Y	S	N
I know which of my team members are at risk of leaving in the next six months.	Y	S	N
We, as a team, find ways to effectively manage stress.	Y	S	N
We openly discuss and encourage boundary setting (like covering each other during vacations, not checking email in the evening unless emergency, etc.)	Y	S	N

When & Where We Work

I am able to offer my team members flexibility while still meeting our business needs.	Y	S	N
I have had a conversation with every team member about what kind of flexibility they need to perform best at work.	Y	S	N
My team members feel trusted and know I don't ever wonder about whether they are working when I can't see them.	Y	S	N
I work flexibly myself (by working at home, flex start time, etc.)	Y	S	N

Work Process

My team members are able to complete their work off-site.   Y   S   N

I consider and approve new ways of doing things in our   Y   S   N
department.

I ask team members to tell me what is wasting time/money at least   Y   S   N
once per quarter.

I give team members autonomy to rethink and redesign how they   Y   S   N
work to be more efficient.

Communication

I openly communicate my commitment to supporting flexibility for   Y   S   N
my team members.

We have tried using a new tech tool to improve communication in   Y   S   N
the last quarter.

I set aside time regularly to talk with team members about   Y   S   N
non-mission-critical things.

I know how to reach every one of my team members in a work   Y   S   N
emergency, even if they are not in the office.

Team Building

We regularly do things as a team to have fun or relieve stress.   Y   S   N

My team members like and respect each other.   Y   S   N

We make it a priority to connect even when we are really busy.   Y   S   N

Add up your score by giving yourself 2 points for a yes answer, 1 point for a maybe/ sometimes and 0 points for a no.

0-20: Make a Change

It takes special skills to lead flexible, remote or dispersed teams. You have good intentions, but the professionals in your organization need more from you as a leader. Identify key areas for growth and commit to making changes that will positively impact both you and your team. Work with HR to request manager training and/or set up a mentorship relationship that will help you learn how to lead in new ways.

21-41: Build Your Skills

You know that work is changing and you need to help your team adjust. But you don't feel like you have the time or energy to draft a Team Alignment Plan and modify work processes. Get started by asking your team members for ideas and support. Seek out managers in your organization or peer associations and ask for best practices and tips to improve your management skills for the new world of work.

42-62: You're Leading the Way

You trust your employees, and you know how to manage their work so that nothing falls through the cracks. You're ready to move ahead with new ways of working. Build your Team Alignment Plan as part of a collaborative team project and continue to check-in with your group on a regular basis.

After you review your overall score, take a look at your results in each sub-section. If you scored well in Team Building but low in Work Process, for example, you'll see where your team could benefit from more focus and innovative thinking.

Tool #1:
Performance

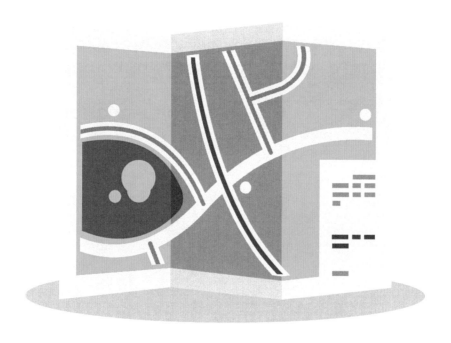

" I think teams need to have clearly defined expectations and this tool is a great way to assist in that process. **"**

- Manager, professional services firm

Tool #1: Performance

Most of us learn how to be managers from the people who managed us. For better or for worse, we develop strengths and bad habits that, over time, become the foundation of our management style.

We find that no matter how long someone has been a manager, many of those original mindsets stick. That means a lot of managers have old attitudes about monitoring performance.

For generations, we've handed down the idea that we have to see people to know they're actually working. Authors Tom Peters and Robert Waterman helped solidify the idea in the 1980s when they popularized the phrase "management by walking around."

Trouble is, face time may not be the best way to manage people...at least not anymore. It's easy to rely on those old school management approaches without realizing the negative impact they can have on team performance. The problem occurs when you have to manage individuals in the new remote/flexible/dispersed workplace—in those situations, your old school approach may actually sabotage your team.

Facing the future of work means looking in the mirror and recognizing the old management attitudes you still carry with you. Recognize that a preference toward working with everyone face to face is really just that, a preference. For every study that shows onsite teams perform better, there's a similar study making the same claim about teams of individuals working virtually.

The key to overcoming your preference for onsite teams is to put a performance system in place that gives you complete transparency about the work getting done, so you can manage for results.

Six Keys to Performance

Here are six areas to think about in terms of how you currently manage for results and how you could improve. If you aren't taking clear, consistent action in each of these areas, you may experience performance breakdowns when your team works in new, dynamic ways.

1. **Identify values and behaviors.** Most organizations are good at communicating their mission, vision, values. But managers don't often think of their own values and how those values shape their expectations of team member behaviors. Getting clear on your values, as well as the behaviors you think should be reflected by team members, will help get your team on the same page. You'll make fewer assumptions about the meaning behind your behaviors, and you'll build trust with each other in the process.

2. **Clarify ownership and autonomy.** As important as this is for onsite teams, it comes into play even more when team members work from multiple locations. Build transparency around everyone's role on the team, and specifically state your expectations around how far their responsibilities extend. Make it clear how far you want them to extend themselves to reach their goals.

3. **Set goals and objectives.** These goals go beyond getting the job done to include professional development, work-life goals and more. Set measurable goals for everyone, especially knowledge workers without immediate deadlines, so that you can clearly evaluate their work.

4. **Monitor performance.** Implement processes that provide enough structure so that you (and other team members) don't wonder what team members are doing if you can't see them working. Good systems replace managing by walking around and face time.

5. **Measure results.** Set measurable goals that are easily and frequently

tracked. Ensure that everyone, no matter their role, has measurable goals, milestones and deadlines by which their work can be judged.

6. **Communicate expectations and hold people accountable.** Clearly communicate your values and behavioral expectations to your team. Hold team members accountable to meet these expectations. Encourage team members to hold each other accountable as well. Build in monitoring systems to facilitate accountability.

Consider these six performance management practices. Which of these do you do well?

_____

_____

_____

Do you already have documented processes for any of these practices?

_____

_____

_____

Where could you be clearer about your expectations?

_____

_____

_____

In which of these areas is your team is the weakest?

_____

_____

_____

_____

What benefits could be achieved by shoring up your performance management practices?

_____

_____

_____

_____

Performance Key #1:
Identify Values and Behaviors

In a new job, it can take three to six months to figure out how your team operates. A new employee needs time to decode things like open/closed door policies, reporting practices, and meeting protocols.

We learn what sociologists call "group norms" from observing the behaviors of our new teammates. And while we're watching and learning, we're not as productive as we could be if someone had let us in on these habits from the beginning. Most of us are never told what is expected with regard to our behavior on a team. We watch and learn what's acceptable or not.

That's what we're talking about here. As a manager, think about the values that are most important to you and how aligned your team could be if you shared those values with them.

Imagine you are going on a week-long camping trip with a bunch of people you don't know. It would be nice to know how you're all going to work together to make the trip a success. Imagine if the leader of the trip started out by indicating his/her values for the trip.

For example, if what you value most as a leader is cooperation, that's a signal about what you expect from each team member on the trip. If the most important value to you is autonomy and self-direction, that sets a very different tone.

But is it enough to identify and communicate your values as a leader? Not really. The word "cooperation" can be played out in team behaviors in many different ways. So can the value of "autonomy." Unless you are clear about your expectations around how each team member should exhibit that value, you're not going to see the behaviors you want.

Consider the assumptions you might make about team members who are working when you can't see them. If they are not behaving in ways that you expect, whose fault is it? Many managers jump to conclusions about remote workers because they don't see the level of visibility or responsiveness they expect. But, if you haven't made your expectations clear, you could have the very best employee letting you down due to a lack of understanding, not because s/he is a slacker.

When asked to identify values, some managers think of them this way:

- We demand hard work, long hours and an unwavering commitment to customer service and satisfaction.

- We understand that sometimes client needs will come before our own.

- We commit to being the industry's pre-eminent experts.

- We recognize that achieving our goals requires each of us to be accountable and dedicated to our team members and clients.

- We will freely share information pertaining to our assignments, schedules, project status, resource needs, obstacles and client needs.

- We take responsibility for managing our time, completing our work and communicating essential information to each other.

- We can feel safe discussing our life needs with co-workers and leaders without reprisal.

- We'll be judged and rewarded based on our performance and the results we achieve, not past behaviors or face time.

- We will respect and support each other's personal needs, style and differences.

Others think of values this way:

- Loyalty
- Honesty
- Integrity
- Discipline

- Trustworthiness
- Fun
- Customer Comes First
- Punctuality

Here are some behaviors you might want to address:

- How quickly team members are expected to reply to voicemails/emails from co-workers, clients, managers, etc.

- How often team members should report their activities and progress toward goals

- How often team members should input information into project tracking systems, customer updates, shared calendar, etc.

- Core hours

- Days/times everyone should be in the office

- Frequency of regularly scheduled team meetings, 1:1 meetings, etc.

- What types of technology you'll use to collaborate in various situations (meetings, brainstorming, virtual coffee breaks, etc.)

- Attendance at retreats

- How decisions will be made and documented

- Conflict-resolution procedures

List three values that are most important to you as a leader—values you believe everyone on your team needs to agree on to be effective.

_____

_____

_____

To identify corresponding behaviors, pick one of the values above and write down three behaviors that your team members should exhibit to reflect their understanding of this value:

1. _____

2. _____

3. _____

You can do the same thing with the other two values here:

_____

_____

_____

_____

When You Say 'Right Away'...

"I'm frustrated when my team members work from home because they're not as responsive as when they're in the office."

A manager expressed responsiveness as her primary value in a recent workshop. It concerned her because she didn't see it reflected in the behaviors of her team members when they worked remotely. When I asked her what does being responsive look like, she responded, "You know, getting back to me right away."

I asked the other managers in the room to tell me what their definition of responsiveness was and I got 13 different answers. One manager said, "Emailing me back within 2 hours." Another, "By the end of the day." A third, "Within the hour."

She realized then that she thought she'd been communicating a behavior (responsiveness) when what she'd be communicating was a value. Without conveying the specific actions she was looking for from her team, she wasn't seeing the results she expected. That's because each person's interpretation of a value can be different. Responsiveness didn't look the same, even among peers she respected.

Challenge yourself to move beyond telling your team they need to "be customer service driven" or "work until the job is done," to defining the specific actions you want to see. You'll start to see signs that work is getting done when your team members reflect your expectations.

 Think about the values and behaviors you'd like to include in your Team Alignment Plan and add them to your draft on page 182.

These are our "rules of engagement" as a team in consideration of our flexible working environment.

1. We are committed to being experts in our field and invest time in reinforcing our subject matter expertise.
2. We will operate within the highest ethical standards when interacting with both internal and external clients, and the team.
3. We will escalate any client service failures immediately to our manager regardless of working status.
4. We will communicate and consider the Client's best interests in determining workplan strategies, timelines, and recommendations on projects.
5. We understand that delivering the most high-quality, thorough and accurate work product sometimes means long hours or extra commitment.
6. We will manage the client's expectations by asking questions regarding desired scope of work, timelines, communication, and availability. We will document and manage the client's requests in these areas to deliver as promised and exceed their expectations.
7. Under all conditions, we will:
   a. Commit to one team meeting per month to review project assignment, revenue, and hold an open discussion regarding team practices, improvements, and needs.
   b. Document engagement deadlines and communicate those deadlines appropriately via email notification, workplan, and calendar updates.
   c. Adhere to internal team policy of completing client project status reports and summary of savings documents by the 5th of each month.
   d. Perform no more than weekly updates to project tracking systems utilized for visibility by the team and supervisors for real-time communication of project status.
   e. Adhere to Firm deadlines regarding time entry, release, and approval; engagement revenue recognition; and project

status updates.

    f. Share information, as permitted by our manager, which is obtained or developed during our engagements to other team members and Firm members to promote knowledge sharing across the organization.

    g. Request feedback and convey appreciation to our clients regarding our engagement progress, onsite fieldwork, and results.

8. We will stay organized on our projects and strive to develop and communicate best practices for use by the team to deliver a standard high-quality work product.

9. We will adhere to Firm and team filing policies to ensure mail and electronically received communication is appropriately stored and visible to pertinent parties.

10. We will apply the utmost protection of client and Firm confidential documentation.

11. We will uphold our responsibility to be mindful of our team members' confidential information and personal conditions.

Here are the ways we agree to keep each other "in the loop" about progress toward our individual and collective goals:

1. One-on-One meetings - these can be live, virtual, or by phone as long as an agenda is prepared and project work plan updates are incorporated and discussed.

2. Project Tracking - this is the team preferred method for managing day-to-day activities, information capture and sharing, progress and needs.

3. Weekly Flash Report - Bullet point email that addresses goals for the week.

    a. Establishes tasks completed, obstacles, and next steps.

    b. This email should be addressed to Manager and copied to all team members to promote knowledge sharing.

Performance Key #2:
Clarify Ownership and Autonomy

As you're building your Team Alignment Plan, review each team member's roles and responsibilities. Go beyond what's in their job descriptions to what you expect of your team members in those roles.

For example, do you expect a more junior person on your team to do "whatever it takes" to get their project deadline met? Or do you have expectations about when you want them to bring you into the process? Sometimes performance breakdowns can occur when a team member doesn't know how far you want them to push, how much you want them to speak their opinions or whether you want to sign off on everything before they move forward.

Helping team members understand these nuances keeps work flowing. This is especially helpful if you're not all in the office at the same time. Tasks are less likely to be put on hold while someone waits for your (or a co-worker's) approval or clarification.

Not clarifying these boundaries can lead to misunderstandings about performance, when the breakdown was really caused by a lack of communication.

What expectations do you have around team member initiative, courage, boundary-setting (or pushing), when to cover you off on things and when to take care of them on their own?

_____

_____

_____

_____

_____

_____

_____

_____

 Think about how you'd like to clarify ownership and autonomy in your Team Alignment Plan and add them to your draft on page 182.

Performance Key #3:
Set Goals and Objectives

Setting goals and objectives is critical to helping you know that everyone on your team is functioning well and work is getting done. For some roles, it seems relatively easy to set measurable goals and objectives. Roles in Customer Service, Quality Assurance, Sales, and Accounting, for example, have very clearly defined goals with metrics and established reporting mechanisms to measure performance.

But managers express more difficulty in how to set goals and objectives for team members with much longer time horizons attached to their projects. The key is to break up projects with longer time spans into shorter more measurable components.

Even if you can't tie specific metrics to those milestones, setting dates and monitoring progress can ensure work is getting done.

When setting goals, don't just think about job performance. You should also set goals for:

- Professional development, such as taking on stretch assignments, presentation skills, joining a board

- Soft skills such as giving feedback, influencing peers, meeting management

- Work-life concerns such as personal wellness, community involvement, family time, taking PTO

What types of individual goals would you like to add for your team? Beyond job performance, what types of goals would you like to set for them?

_____

_____

_____

_____

_____

_____

_____

 Add your goal setting notes to your Team Alignment Plan on page 182.

Performance Key #4:
Monitor Performance

Think about the ways you currently monitor team performance, especially when you can't see them working. Monitoring individual performance is the simplest way to let go of managing by face time and walking around. Challenge yourself to think differently.

Many factors influence how managers monitor team member progress. Depending on schedules, work style and communication preferences, time zones and type of work, you may prefer more verbal or written forms of monitoring.

CC We don't look over employees' shoulders when we are in the office, so why do we micromanage teleworkers? **>>**

- Manager, state transportation agency

Set up monitoring systems for everyone on your team, no matter where they work. That way no one will feel singled out and everyone's performance can improve.

Here are four popular ways that managers monitor performance:

Flash Report: This three-part email briefly recaps work completed, obstacles to completing work and work to be done next. (See sample in the back of this book.)

Project Plan/Project Management Software: This tool tracks work to be done, deadlines, responsible parties and status of deliverables. Software helps monitor progress, assign tasks and store related documents.

Departmental Reports: Standardized department reports track job progress.

One-on-one Meetings (live, virtual or by phone): Hold regular status meetings or block off time each week for open office hours when everyone knows you're available for pre-scheduled or impromptu meetings.

We all know that leadership is situational, but charting your natural default as a leader can help you balance your need to trust or control your team members.

If you are on the trust end of the continuum, you may need to put more structure in place to reduce crises that could occur from assuming work is getting done on time and at the level of quality you expect. Managing to a project plan and holding regular status and/or project meetings is key.

If you're more on the control end, then you need to question your rationale. If your team member is a proven performer, rein yourself in. Tell yourself, "I've got to remember to trust this individual and manage to their results." Not surprisingly, tools like project plans and status meetings can help you here too. They give you "eyes and ears" on the ground, so that you can be assured the project is running smoothly.

Where are you on the
TRUST-CONTROL
CONTINUUM?

TRUST

Do you tend to trust your employees?
"Hey, you're a grownup. You know how to get your job done. You're skilled at what you do. So good luck! Check in with me once it's time to turn things in."

CONTROL

Are you a manager who needs to be measuring and watching how people are actually working?

How would you like your team members to communicate with you about their progress toward deadlines, milestones and goals?

_____

_____

_____

How would you like your team members to communicate with each other about their progress?

_____

_____

_____

How often?

_____

_____

How can you change the way you work to focus more on results than facetime?

_____

_____

_____

Here are the ways we agree to keep each other "in the loop" about progress toward our individual and collective goals:

1. One-on-One meetings - these can be live, virtual, or by phone as long as an agenda is prepared and project work plan updates are incorporated and discussed.
2. Project Tracking - this is the team preferred method for managing day-to-day activities, information capture and sharing, progress and needs.
3. Weekly Flash Report - This bullet point email addresses goals for the week.
   a. Establishes tasks completed, obstacles, and next steps.
   b. This email should be addressed to Manager and copied to all team members to promote knowledge sharing.

SAMPLE: MONITORING AND MEASURING RESULTS

Write down your ideas about how to monitor performance in your Team Alignment Plan on page 182.

Performance Key #5:
Measure Results

Goals for each of your team members need to be measurable. You can do this by assigning quantitative metrics like these:

- Speed-to-shelf
- Net promoter scores
- Decrease in customer complaints
- Revenue, sales, profits
- $ collected, invoiced, applied
- On-time (or early) delivery
- Increased availability or coverage
- Reduced costs
- Deals closed
- Increased membership, site visits, orders, attendees
- Improved quality
- Decreased time/cost to hire, absenteeism, turnover
- Fewer discrepancies, mistakes, bugs, recalls
- Higher safety scores

Or, assigning timelines and due dates like this:

A project manager working from home may be in charge of the deployment of a new customer solution at the end of the year. How do you know if s/he is working effectively day to day? You might:

1. Break the project into smaller units of work with milestones every month or so.

2. Document the project using a project plan that outlines the project manager's responsibilities and due dates.

3. Meet weekly to review progress and address potential obstacles.

4. Encourage the project manager to submit a flash report weekly (see page

192) to you and the team so that there's visibility into the work getting done.

5. Check in with co-workers and the client from time to time to get feedback on the project manager's performance.

Are you setting goals based on quantitative metrics or timelines?

_____

_____

Are there opportunities to be more specific about team members' goals?

_____

_____

Are your goals always SMART (see sidebar) or could you do a better job of that?

_____

_____

What can you do to sharpen your goals and objectives in a way that will give you a better "line of sight" into what everyone on your team is doing?

_____

_____

_____

Smart Goals

SMART is an acronym for **Specific, Measurable, Attainable, Results-oriented,** and **Time-bound.**

For example, if a team member needs to increase sales calls, the SMART goal might be stated as follows: By the end of the first quarter, I will have increased my sales calls by 15% over the same quarter last year. If someone is lacking the professional development needed for advancement, his/her SMART goal might be: In the next twelve months I will complete the four classes required for certification in my field.

Review individual and team goals to make sure they are truly SMART. Record milestone dates for these goals on your calendar. If an employee needs more coaching and oversight, you might need to break down these goals into smaller action steps with their own due dates.

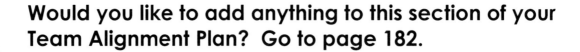

Would you like to add anything to this section of your Team Alignment Plan? Go to page 182.

Performance Key #6:
Communicate Expectations and Hold People Accountable

Holding people accountable is another specific challenge managers face when managing dispersed teams. Think about how to improve accountability, no matter where people work.

Specify outcomes. Asking "Can you have this done by Friday?" is ripe for misinterpretation. Clarify what "done" means. It could mean a draft is complete, that it's final and ready for approval, or that it has been approved, or that it's been approved and posted to your intranet site. Be clear about what you expect the outcome to be.

Identify boundaries. Managers have very different expectations about whether they want to be cc'd on every email from their team members or only the most important ones. One manager will expect their team member to let them know at the first sign of a problem, another will only expect you to tell them if you need his/her help resolving it. Be clear about your expectations around how far team members should push, report back to you, raise issues to clients, etc.

Provide a time frame. Define what the end of the day (or week) means for your global team. Be specific and set group norms for the time zone you'll default to, or the standard definition you'll use for end of the week. Set deadlines for every task and encourage team members to negotiate deadlines if not explicitly stated.

Confirm understanding. Go out of your way to confirm someone's understanding of the work you've delegated to them. This is particularly important when you can't read non-verbals or seek confirmation face to face. Don't just send an email and cross your fingers. Encourage everyone on your team to do the same.

Create a feedback loop. Determine the types of projects that require debrief meetings and the frequency and location of those meetings. Agree together on how best to provide feedback. Put systems in place for getting feedback from clients and others on matrixed teams, so that you can constantly be improving.

Instill confidence. Help team members know why you may be pushing them outside of their comfort zone on a project. Giving them additional exposure without instilling confidence and providing context can lead to misunderstandings.

The key is to do this consistently (as in every day, every meeting, every call) and to encourage team members to hold each other accountable to the process. That means if you, as the manager, fail to set a deadline, a team member should prompt you for one.

What could you and your team members do to better hold each other accountable?

_____

_____

_____

What kind of feedback loops do you have or do you want to create to make sure that information is being circulated in a way that leads to individual and team performance improvements?

_____

_____

_____

Do your team members understand clearly what is expected of them?
How do you know they understand?

_____

_____

_____

Have you gotten their feedback on your expectations and reached agreement on how to handle roadblocks and complications?

_____

_____

_____

 Note any additional ideas about performance on page 182.

What's The Real Goal?

A manager thought he did a good job of managing performance. He made sure team members wrote goals each year and held them accountable for achieving those goals. He saw himself as a role model... until he got feedback from his team.

They told him that he needed to get real with himself about what he thought constituted good performance. That's because when it came time to evaluating and differentiating the performance of his team members at the end of each year, decisions weren't being made based on whether or not people achieved their goals.

Instead, performance evaluations seemed to be based on some qualitative measures (values) the manager believed were important to the team's success—things like conflict resolution, being proactive, positive client feedback, etc.

He realized that he had failed to communicate the yardstick he was really using to measure results. Making this adjustment helped his team's performance because they all knew what they were really working toward, rather than going through the motions of goal-setting and performance management.

Tool #2:
Capacity & Resiliency

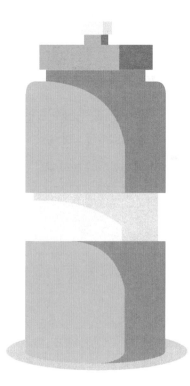

" By letting employees work from home when they couldn't get to the office due to weather and mild illness, we found that the team saved 32 hours in productivity. "

- Manager, state transportation agency

Tool #2: Capacity & Resiliency

If your main focus as a manager is to push team members to work as hard as they can for as long as they can without consideration for their lives, their health or well-being, you're not doing your job.

Your organization should be putting you in charge of *optimizing* resources, not maximizing them. They've provided you with the appropriate process, labor, and equipment, and now they're holding you responsible for delivering a return on that investment.

Unfortunately, many leaders think their job is to *maximize* resources. So they work employees into the ground with little concern for the cost of disengagement, stress, absenteeism and turnover...and little concern for diminished returns when employee are overworked.

There's a big difference between maximizing and optimizing resources. And it's up to you to help leaders in your organization understand the difference.

Maximizing resources means squeezing every last drop of value out of a resource to get maximum output or performance. *Optimizing* resources means finding the right balance between energy input and performance output.

Energy input is part capacity (how many hours your employees can work) and part resiliency (how well can employees bounce back from stress to put quality energy into the work they do). Optimizing resources means you're managing both employee capacity and resiliency to get the best possible performance.

Collectively, we've forgotten about resiliency. Pushed to do more with less for years now, employees are maxed out. Most managers have considered resiliency strategies a luxury and have not fully acknowledged the impact of their "maximization" strategy on the workforce. The result is a labor force that is less productive, more stressed, and disengaged:

- In the U.S., employee engagement declined 3 percentage points between 2011 and 2012, even though GDP held steady. Looking longer term, engagement dropped 5 percentage points between 2009 and 2012.[1]

- In 2013, a leading EAP provider found that stress had jumped to employees' #2 health concern (behind losing weight). The percentage of employees ranking stress as their top concern jumped from 18% to 26% in just one year.[2]

Managing Workload

One of the most asked questions we hear from managers is "How can I motivate employees, especially people who have worked here a long time?" I always wish I could tell them something simple that would fix it, or share some pixie dust with magical powers. That seems to be what they're looking for.

But pixie dust and magic powers can't change the way our workforce has been living—overworked and stressed out—for years.

Instead, I can tell you that making systemic changes to the way you and your team manage your workload and improve employee resiliency will improve engagement and productivity. In the National Workplace Flexibility Study, engagement measures in one participating company increased 7 percentage points. At the same company, 43% of managers indicated that team productivity increased after completing our Team Alignment Plan.

By honestly evaluating the amount of work individuals on your team can handle (capacity), you will improve the output (performance) of your team and help them become more resilient. This will reduce the amount of stress your team members experience and will increase motivation and engagement.

---

1 2013 Trends in Global Employee Engagement, Aon Hewitt
2 ComPsych: Tell It Now poll, January 2013

What exactly is resiliency? It's the ability to bounce back from stress and adversity. It impacts your team members' health, concentration, energy, attention and strength. It's what influences how much energy an employee can give to his/her work.

Some work-life experts stress that it's important for individuals to own their own resiliency. I don't disagree that it's a factor, but I believe that managers (and ultimately your organization's leaders) strongly influence employee resiliency. An individual can control his/her response to stress, but managers can control (and sometimes are) the source of stress.

Making an investment in team capacity and resiliency is not about being nice. It's about improving performance.

Let's start with steps you can take to improve employee capacity. Then we'll move on to resiliency.

Managing Capacity

Recent studies show that team members feel more productive and are healthier when they have more control over their schedules and are able to work from home, even occasionally.

But you probably already know this from personal experience. Where do you go to get some good thinking time, to finish a big project, or do some writing? You probably work from home.

When we work flexibly, individual capacity improves. But for managers, flexible work environments can decrease our ability to measure employee capacity. You can't tell on a conference call whether a team member is rolling his eyes, sighing or getting anxious as you delegate work.

One of the most important parts of your job as manager is to play "traffic cop" with your department's work. Not only do you need to monitor individual workloads and redistribute work, you need to help everyone on your team prioritize and run interference with clients when deadlines are at risk.

You need to have a line of sight into all of the moving parts of your team, but that can be difficult. And managing by walking around or dropping in on people to monitor their workload isn't always the most effective strategy to accomplish this.

Managing workload is hard enough when everyone works together onsite. So when you work on a dispersed team, it's imperative that you have systems in place to monitor capacity. Strategies include:

- **Resource management:** Calculate the total number of person-hours you have available and the number of hours of work. Share the gap with your team to ask for suggestions for how to close the gap (by renegotiating scope, shifting deadlines, asking for additional resources, removing low value components of the project). Share the gap with your leadership and the strategies you're using to try to close the gap.

- **Priority management:** Given the amount of time each team member has available and looking at the tasks on their to-do list, help them make tough decisions about their attendance in meetings, the priority of each of the tasks, what to delegate, what to abandon, etc.

- **Deadline setting:** We tend to overestimate client expectations. Encourage all of your team members to request deadlines from clients (internal and external) rather than making assumptions or being the first to suggest a deadline date. Then renegotiate those deadlines when necessary.

- **Time management:** Encourage team members to attend fewer meetings, send fewer emails, stop copying everyone on emails, take vacation and spend time connecting with others. Hold them accountable for making tough choices and not trying to "do it all."

- **Monitoring their happiness quotient:** It's okay if your team is working beyond capacity sometimes, but advanced notice helps, as does acknowledging the challenges of working beyond capacity. Check in with team members to see how they're doing and encourage honesty.

- **Resource balancing:** At any given time, some of your team members may have too much on their plate and others not enough. Be flexible enough to adjust individual workloads when capacity levels aren't balanced.

- **Stop managing by crisis:** Some managers love a good crisis—somehow all that last-minute panic makes us feel important. There's nothing like a crisis to rally your team, but over time you lose credibility and your team loses resiliency. Kick the crisis addiction and reward team members when they prevent a crisis through strong communication and good planning.

Tools for planning, monitoring, and managing workload and capacity:

- Use project plans and meet as a project team to discuss progress toward milestones and deadlines.

- Keep a master spreadsheet on which each team member logs the percentage of time spent on their main tasks or projects. Monitor weekly and adjust to level-set workloads.

- Set up one-on-one meetings strictly devoted to helping team members prioritize tasks.

- RACI diagrams help you see when a team member has put themselves in too many decision making roles. Challenge their need to be in every meeting or have a hand in every decision.

- Provide feedback on the amount of work your team members are recording in their flash reports. Suggest ways to resolve overwork situations.

- Review your processes and have contests that reward employees for redesigning an inefficient work practice in favor of a low/no cost, more efficient approach.

- Organize teams of employees to be incubators for innovative approaches that apply to the work you're currently doing.

More tips for managing capacity and avoiding chronic overwork:

- Meet regularly with team members to discuss workload.

- Set expectations around workload so that team members can anticipate the ebbs and flows of their work on each of their projects.

- Discuss client and project needs regularly with your team members so they can plan their personal lives accordingly.

- Work with team members to determine how best to meet both client and team member needs around flexibility. Many times they will see different opportunities than you do.

- Encourage boundary setting, even with customers.

- Say no when possible.

- Help clients understand the cost benefit of additional project requests so they can make an educated decision about whether their request is worth it or not. Don't just say yes to every request.

- When you do accept additional work, explain to the team the reasons for accepting and the benefits to the group.

- Encourage employees to ask for (and renegotiate) deadlines.

- Ask employees to tell you when they're feeling overwhelmed or want more work to do.

- Take time to debrief projects and help team members see what worked and what didn't.

- Encourage team members to work together to forge solutions to make projects or tasks more efficient.

- Be realistic about your own capacity. If team members see you being unrealistic about your own workload, your commitment to their capacity management might be questioned.

- Challenge employees if you hear them being unrealistic about their capacity vs. their workload.

- Watch for warning signs of overwork (deadlines slipping, communication decreasing, missing appointments).

- Encourage team members to speak up when they find themselves challenging the value of the work they're doing. Tell them you want them to suggest eliminating low value work or propose more efficient ways to do the work they currently have.

- Cross train teams in order to encourage better client coverage.

- Hire contingent workers if possible.

- Encourage and model delegation.

- Meet regularly to discuss and negotiate priorities. Go so far as to ask team members to bring their "to-do" list with them and work through the tasks one by one, ranking them as a level 1, 2, or 3 priority. Over time, this should help them learn what matters most to you and prioritize on their own.

- Set priorities based on reality, and encourage your leadership to do the same.

- Openly discuss and negotiate priorities and resource constraints with your leadership.

- Challenge the prevailing leadership attitude of "I know we don't have enough people but get it done anyway" by repeatedly bringing resource constraints to the attention of your leadership.

Negotiating Boundaries

A director was having a stressful day (feeling like she and her team were beyond capacity and they just kept getting more and more requests), when a co-worker asked for a project report. This director snapped at her co-worker saying, "I have too much on my plate right now. I can't possibly get you this until tomorrow!"

That's when the co-worker said her hope was to get it sometime within the month, not today or tomorrow. As a result, the director realized that she makes assumptions about deadlines instead of simply asking.

Taking note, she changed her approach and has seen a big difference. Her team is not nearly as overloaded because she isn't turning everything into a fire drill anymore.

Managing Capacity With Clients

Good client management is about working in a transparent way with both internal and external clients. Discuss the logistics of the project management process, before the engagement begins, to clarify their expectations and communicate the way you work.

Consider this a peer-to-peer negotiation. We tend to make the mistake of thinking of clients like parents, and ourselves as a child trying to please our parent by doing whatever it takes. This is an outdated attitude that can lead to overwork and burnout.

Here is a checklist of topics to cover in that initial meeting:

- ☐ Ideal deadline for the project, and appropriate milestones
- ☐ Frequency of status update meetings
- ☐ Preferred method and frequency of communication
- ☐ Revision process, decision makers, rounds of reviews, who makes the final call
- ☐ Number of team members, roles, who'll be onsite/offsite and the frequency
- ☐ Which meetings, deliverables and/or phases of the project will need to be conducted in person and which can be done over the phone or in a video conference
- ☐ Process for handling out-of-scope requests, revision process, decision makers, length of time needed for various aspects of the project
- ☐ Standing vacation requests, conferences and other events that will prevent work during those times

Which tools or strategies would you like to use with your team to monitor workload?

_____

_____

_____

_____

How can you "keep each other honest" when it comes to managing expectations about workload?

_____

_____

_____

_____

Is overwork an issue for your team? What can you do to address it?

_____

_____

_____

_____

How are you going to change the way you manage your customers to reduce stress from things like last minute deadlines, scope creep and unrealistic expectations?

_____

_____

_____

What are some ways you may be able to create more capacity or better coverage for your team?

_____

_____

_____

 Note your ideas for managing workload in your Team Alignment Plan at the back of the book.

Resiliency

Capacity and resiliency go hand in hand. But while managing for capacity is more clearly linked to workload and deadline issues, managing for resiliency requires a more interpersonal, soft skills approach. You can boost resiliency by helping team members find value in the work they do and encouraging them to make purposeful work-life choices.

Managers can improve team resiliency by focusing on these strategies:

- Provide more options for team members to choose where and when they work.

- Encourage team members to set a work-life goal, and then hold them accountable.

- Offer work-life coaching to help team members implement resiliency strategies.

- Give people the time and space to practice resiliency strategies.

- Give people opportunities to develop their careers and leadership abilities through stretch assignments or high visibility projects, if they're interested.

- Encourage team members to take risks and celebrate mistakes as learning opportunities.

- Create opportunities for people to connect on a personal level through team-building moments.

- Spend time together in person.

- Find ways to link the work the team is doing to the bigger picture. Show how their work supports company goals and contributes to society.

- Provide regular feedback.

- Encourage and model boundary setting.

- Delay-send emails you draft late at night or on weekends.

- Intervene when flight-risk employees show signs of burnout.

- Put personal commitments on your shared calendar and encourage team members to provide more information than "appointment" to share what they really have going on.

- Volunteer together in your community, or encourage individual volunteerism, and then schedule time for team members to share their experiences.

- Celebrate achievements.

- Let go of perfectionism; practice "good, better, best."

- Build in time on your project plans for professionals to take their PTO.

- Take your PTO and encourage team members to use all of theirs.

- Build in coverage through cross-training, so team members don't need to work during PTO.

Encourage Team Members to Take PTO

Studies show that we improve our well-being (and productivity) by taking time away from work. Researcher Mark Rosekind of Alertness Solutions found that a vacation can increase reaction time by 30% to 40% even after the trip is over. Iowa State professor Wallace Huffman says a holiday can boost productivity by 60% for a month or two following vacation.

But many of us have grown accustomed to working on vacation, so how can you stop?

Choice #1: Go cold turkey

Clearly communicate to everyone around you the value of taking PTO, and then break the news that you will not be available on your upcoming vacation. Let everyone know in plenty of time to plan ahead and develop workarounds. Agree on the best way to reach you in the case of a real emergency.

Take a deep breath and go for it. You'll be amazed at the results!

Choice #2: Scale back slowly

If you're used to being available all day, every day, start with being unavailable for one whole day. Or tell everyone you'll respond only to the most urgent emails between 8:30-10:30 a.m.

Agree on one technology your team will use with you in a true emergency.
Set subject line conventions in email to make it easier to scan your inbox quickly.

Take the time to establish rules in Outlook so that Reply All emails go in a separate folder to make it easier to scan your inbox while you're out. Communicate with your clients and your team about your limited availability on vacation.

Find a colleague with whom to trade coverage. You cover them on their vacation; they'll cover you on yours.

Declare to your vacation partners (friend, family, dog!) that you will not be working for certain periods of time during vacation, so they can keep you honest.

Conveniently forget your smartphone in your hotel room for blocks of time, and see what happens when you get back. Did anyone really miss you? Did a crisis really occur?

Vacations are Good for Your Health

A nine-year study tracked 12,000 middle-aged men and found that taking an annual vacation is associated with reduced risk of death due to heart disease. (Journal Psychosomatic Medicine, 2000)

Failing to take a break at least once a year increases psychological health issues in women. The risk of depression increases as the frequency of vacations decline. (Wisconsin Medical Journal, 2005)

Simply leaving the office isn't good enough...not if you have your BlackBerry in hand. According to researchers at the Faculty of Management at Tel Aviv University, people who remain connected to the office don't get the same vacation benefits as those who leave work behind.

Are You a Model of Resiliency?

Your own personal work-life decisions can impact employee resiliency. For example, if you tell everyone on your team not to work on vacation, and then you do, it sends the wrong message.

Ask yourself whether you're role modeling the right resiliency habits:

- Do you send emails in the middle of the night?
- Do you work at the expense of your health, family or sanity?
- Do you routinely skip social, spiritual or physical workout opportunities in favor of working?
- Do you take PTO, work at home or openly discuss your own work-life needs?
- Do you work through vacation?
- Do you set and communicate work-life goals?
- Do you make values-based decisions to prioritize your actions?

- Are you aware of the messages your behavior conveys to those around you?
- What non-verbal messages do you send about the "right" way to be successful?
- Are you giving team members "permission" to discuss work and life issues freely?

What factors negatively impact resiliency on your team?

_____

_____

_____

What strategies do you want to try to improve resiliency?

_____

_____

_____

How will you monitor employee burnout?

_____

_____

_____

How will you encourage your team to take PTO?

_____

_____

_____

Record other ideas here:

_____

_____

_____

_____

_____

Link Work to the Bigger Picture

One manager improves team resiliency by always explaining the "WHY" behind her decisions and the work her team is doing. She finds that if employees can see the link between their work and the organization's bigger picture priorities, team members feel less stressed and more energized.

She also tries to find each employee's "passion points" and assigns them to projects that open up opportunities to do what they love or are best at.

1. We will not "over-promise" and commit ourselves to unrealistic deadlines. We will request deadlines from internal and external clients and then negotiate delivery based on the resources we have available.

2. We maintain relationships with independent contractors so that we can ramp up and down as our workload fluctuates. Team members will help manage workload by asking for freelance help when their work expands beyond capacity.

3. Each team member will set an annual work-life goal. Team members will review those goals with their manager as part of a quarterly review meetings and will receive an incentive for meeting that goal.

4. As a team, we aim for at least 90% utilization of our PTO time each year. The team will be treated to a catered lunch and each member will receive a company apparel item of their choice when we hit that goal.

Add your capacity and resiliency considerations on the draft of your Team Alignment Plan on page 183.

Tool #3:
When & Where We Work

“ This is a great tool to initiate discussion and achieve a focused commitment on the activity of flex. It has allowed it to be routine in the way that we work because we thought of the pitfalls early. And, as the manager, I was able to set some very clear boundaries relative to client service delivery. **”**

- Manager, biotech company

Tool #3: When & Where We Work

Workplace wars are on the rise. Some organizations are doubling down on real estate and redesigning their onsite offices to include upscale dining facilities, coffee shops and touchdown spaces where individuals and teams can meet.

Others are reducing or eliminating office space to increase the proportion of time employees spend working from home or in third places.

Still others recognize the value of both and encourage mobility for their employees, so that when it makes sense to be in the office, you come in. When it makes sense to work remotely, you do that.

You may be looking at the impact of these types of workplace changes on your team:

- Hoteling spaces
- Open plan office environments
- Third spaces (coffee houses, co-working spaces, etc.)
- Flexible work
- Telework

- Internal mobility (freedom to choose your workspace anywhere on your company's campus)
- Dispersed teams across office locations, country or the world
- Total mobility to work anytime, anywhere

Circle the ones that could be options for your team or write them here:

_____

_____

_____

When making the decision about what's right for you, consider an integrated approach where Real Estate and Facilities Management, Human Resources, Information Technology and Leadership all work together to recommend a solution. Managers and employees at every level should provide feedback, helping a holistic workplace solution to emerge.

Too often, without this integrated approach, workplace strategy decisions are made based on the comfort level of senior leadership. That's exactly the wrong way to approach a decision that has far reaching implications on the success of the organization.

Opening the rules about how, where and when people work can unleash team productivity, engagement and effectiveness. That might seem strange if you see workplace change as a potential impediment to productivity.

How do you feel about changing the rules around where and when team members work?

_____

_____

_____

_____

Redefining Workplace Flexibility

Traditionally, workplace flexibility conjured up images of everyone working at home with no one left to answer the phone on Fridays and turn out the lights. Today's definition of workplace flexibility is a whole lot more complex. It refers to enabling employees to have the flexibility to work where and when they need to based on the task they're doing, who they're meeting with, and their obligations outside of work. It incorporates a range of onsite and offsite options.

Admittedly, there are challenges to managing teams this way. Many of the suggestions in this book involve overcoming the challenges of dispersed teams. But the same strategies are applicable to employees working in all of these other workplaces as well. Even when teams work in very traditional ways, the strategies in this book can help you improve performance and trust.

We encourage you to think about whatever workplace challenge you are facing and apply the principles in this book to that situation, whether it fits the traditional definition of flexibility or not.

When it comes to flexibility in the workplace, 15 years of data has proven the value to organizations.

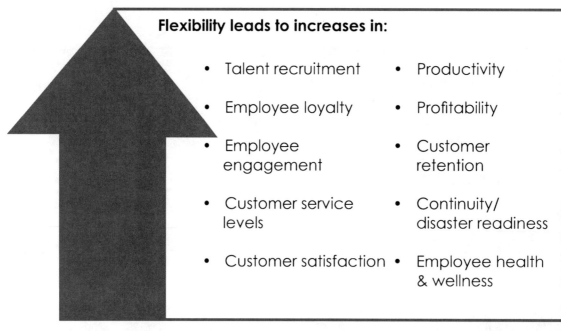

Flexibility leads to increases in:

- Talent recruitment
- Employee loyalty
- Employee engagement
- Customer service levels
- Customer satisfaction

- Productivity
- Profitability
- Customer retention
- Continuity/ disaster readiness
- Employee health & wellness

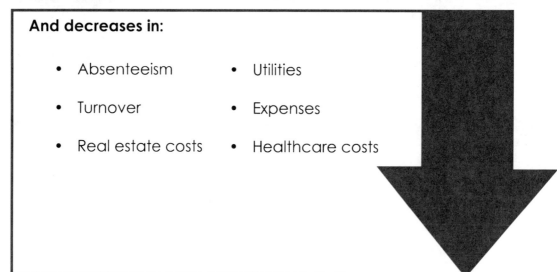

And decreases in:

- Absenteeism
- Turnover
- Real estate costs

- Utilities
- Expenses
- Healthcare costs

There are so many ways to think differently about when and where team members work. Get creative! Even roles that require employees to work onsite can be flexible. Here are some of the many ways flexibility can be defined:

- Flex time & place
- Regular or short-notice flex time
- Telework
- Compressed workweeks
- Job sharing
- Flex careers
- Sabbaticals
- Dialing careers up & down
- Gradual return to work
- Phased retirement
- Reduced time
- Part time
- Part-year work

- Time off & unpaid leave
- Comp time
- Paid vacations & sick leave
- Choices in managing time
- Self-scheduling / online scheduling
- Shift trading
- Team scheduling
- Floaters
- Redesigning overtime rules
- No fault attendance policy
- Leave banks
- PTO in less than 8-hour shifts

Consider:

1. Needs of the business
2. Department limitations
3. Nature of the position
4. Individual work style
5. Individual performance

Consider how improving team flexibility could impact your coverage needs, too.

Flex can help you improve team performance and availability! You can expand coverage to accommodate time zones and internal/external customer needs. A receptionist who starts and ends his/her day earlier (or later) can provide phone coverage for customers on the coasts. Meetings with global teams that take place at night are easier to manage when team members don't have to report into work by the standard start time.

Rethink the Norm

We hear lots of managers brag about how flexible they are and how much flexibility is woven into the fabric of their team. After all, they give employees as much flexibility as they want if they have doctor appointments, are sick or have childcare needs.

But these managers use a definition of flexibility that is more about their willingness to go with the flow rather than leveraging new ways of work to produce better results.

Rather than considering every team member's request individually, as an exception to normal business practices, look at the positive impact of rethinking where and when team members work. Individuals always have things going on that require them to need some flexibility—build that in as the norm. It's just the way you need to do business today.

Tips for Working Successfully in Open Plan and Hoteling Concepts

- Take advantage of the different options your workspace provides and take note of the spaces your team tends to gravitate toward. Challenge yourself to try new work areas even if they don't seem appealing at first.

- Avoid squatting. Team members might be tempted to always reserve a conference room for quiet or reserve the same workspace every day. The point of these design concepts is for everyone to try new things.

- Don't be afraid of the noise. Workspace designers know how to intentionally use white noise to make conversation noises less distracting.

- Try hanging out together in collaborative spaces. Work independently but in the company of others. This can promote impromptu conversation and information sharing you won't get in a personal workspace.

- Implement monthly workspace debrief sessions to communicate what's working and what's not in your new space. This will help you clarify expectations and agree on ways to overcome challenges.

- Agree that it's okay to tell someone what you're really thinking. If a team member is talking on the phone in a quiet space, say something. If someone works with headphones in and zones out so it's impossible to get their attention, say something. If keyboards in your hoteling space are consistently covered with crumbs or you see someone not wiping down a shared workstation at the end of the day, say something!

- As a manager, resist the urge to over-monitor team members' comings and goings. Just because you can see them doesn't mean that everything they do is your business. Don't comment about their third trip to the coffee bar—it can make them self-conscious.

- Share your work style preferences so that team members know how others feel about interruptions, disruptions and the visibility that comes with your workspace. Be respectful of each other's preferences.

- Agree how you'll integrate technology with your open plan environment so that remote employees still feel connected. Don't fall into bad habits of not including them because they're not in the same location as you.

Are you open to flexible work schedules for your team? Why or why not?

_____

_____

_____

What are the specific restrictions that your department requires on how, where and when team members can work?

_____

_____

_____

Do you experience service interruptions, project delays or unnecessary downtime when team members are sick, on vacation or working flexibly?

_____

_____

_____

Considering everyone's roles, the needs of your business, and your clients, what types of flex might be possible?

_____

_____

_____

Team-Based Flexibility

Team-based flexibility is a new way of thinking that helps you position the decisions about where and when team members are working as a *business process*. Your organization's policies and workplace design strategies set the parameters for your team as to what is possible. Individuals express their needs and desires, and you, as a manager, control an outcome that works for the entire group

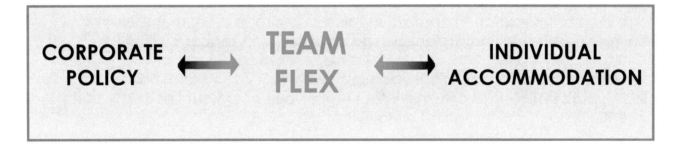

Here's how it works:

1. Identify the types of flexibility that could work for your team.
2. Start a conversation with team members about what you think is possible.
3. Tell them that you're supportive of thinking differently about where and when they work.
4. Invite them to talk with you individually about flexibility needs over the next few weeks.
5. With this information, consider what is possible within the desires of your team members.
6. Provide feedback about how you all can make it work, or
7. Encourage team members to work together to problem solve if their combined needs are going to conflict.

You may think you know what flexibility your team wants based on who's asked you for flex. But studies show that many people who would like to work flexibly are too afraid to ask.

Proactively approach your team so you can identify interest and consider the needs of the whole team, rather than individual piecemeal requests.

By engaging your team in a conversation about options and business needs, you can tap into their ideas about how flexibility could work. Their solutions may surprise you.

Reason-Neutral Flexibility

If an employee wants to work in new ways, you should consider his/her request, regardless of the reason. In fact, you should discourage team members from sharing any personal motivations behind a flexible work request.

Otherwise, the reason could put you in an awkward position and make your decision subjective. Not only might that make you uncomfortable, but it could potentially open your organization to risks of perceived bias.

How did it feel to have a pro-active conversation with your team about their flexibility needs? Anything surprise you?

_____

_____

_____

What requests did you get from your team members?

_____

_____

_____

_____

Was it difficult to remain reason-neutral, why or why not?

_____

_____

_____

_____

SAMPLE: WHEN & WHERE WE WORK

1. Staff can work a maximum of two days a week from home.
2. All team members are required to work in the office on Thursdays.
3. We will update our calendar to establish days we are working remotely to help meeting organizers who are relying on calendar information.
4. We strive to cover every team member's flexibility needs and expect the same coverage for ourselves in return.

Considering all of this, what do you want to address in your Team Alignment Plan about where and when your team can work. Write down your thoughts on page 183.

Tool #4:
Work Process

" This process even works in matrixed teams! I didn't think it could be done, but people are coming together cross-functionally now to share ideas that make our processes more efficient. Our internal clients are happier than ever. "

- Manager, food manufacturer

Tool #4: Work Process

Teams often continue to work the same way they always have, despite changing customer needs, technology, resources, organizational priorities and team member skill sets.

When was the last time you and your team evaluated the way work is getting done to establish new procedures and let go of low-value work?

Not surprisingly, many employees are restricted from telework because their job requires them to be where the paper is, or where the people are, or where the specialized equipment is, or where the whiteboards are.

What, whiteboards? Yes, sometimes it's a simple restriction like a file drawer or a whiteboard that prevents team members from working remotely.

Workplace change can be a catalyst for teams to rethink how they work. It gives you an opportunity to rethink the ways you have always done things. If you're moving into a new office space, for example, you have an opportunity to try out new tools and spaces and rethink the ways you've collaborated or worked together in the past.

It's also an invitation to eliminate busy work, like reports that no one reads, filing hard copies, and other no/low value work that takes time and diminishes productivity.

We know of one manufacturer that openly encourages every employee to discuss the 20% of their work that will never get done. Consider how powerful a tool that could be for you to improve engagement and productivity. Even if you could strategically eliminate 10% of low value work processes, your productivity and resiliency would skyrocket!

Working at 80%

An administrative assistant who wanted to reduce her hours to 80% of full time made her employer nervous. How could they say yes to this request when she had more than enough work to do in her full-time role?

Easy! She inventoried all of the work she was responsible for, identified redundancies and inefficiencies, and recommended the elimination of some low value work.

Through the process, she eliminated 20% of her role while still doing everything that the staff needed her to do.

Work processes that may need to be redesigned:

Knowledge transfer	Supervising
Answering phones	Customer/client coverage
Collaboration	Brainstorming
Training	Problem solving
Scheduling	Meeting management
Filing	Document approvals
Document sharing	Onboarding

Work Process Redesign Chart

To use this chart, start by listing the work processes you want to redesign. Then, identify your current approach in Column 1, the negative impact on your team in Column 2, and ways to do it differently in Column 3.

	Current	Impact	New
Work Process: MEETINGS	Casually discuss agenda in advance.	Remote employees don't always have input into the agenda.	Ask for agenda items 48 hours in advance, publish agenda 24 hours in advance.
	Meetings start 10 minutes late while we wait for everyone.	Waste of time, time is money.	All meetings will be 50 minutes long to leave time to get to next meeting or set up technology. Meetings start on time.
	We start meetings by asking if everyone has read the supporting documents and summarize if everyone is not up to speed.	Wastes time and discourages attendees from prepping in advance since they know we'll cover it anyway.	We agree that everyone will prep for meeting in advance. If not, the meeting will continue as if you have.
	We meet in a conference room with a speaker phone for remote team members to dial in.	Remote employees can't always hear or feel left out when they're forgotten on the call.	We vary meetings between conference room and dial-in number with everyone calling in from their work station. We bring tent cards with names of remote employees to the conference room with us, so that we remember they're on the call.
	Scribe is appointed at every meeting and distributes meeting notes via email afterwards.	Takes a lot of extra time and fills up inboxes with more emails.	Leader takes notes real time in the meeting and displays the document for attendees to see. After the meeting, those notes are saved to a file on the shared drive.

Too Close to the Process

The VP of Finance in a professional services firm was adamant that his two accounting clerks could not work remotely. When asked why, he replied, "Our filing process for invoices involves printing them in duplicate and filing the copies in two binders that sit in a cubicle behind their desks." He had looked into automating their billing system and it was going to cost in the high five-figures so that was not an option.

Not wanting to call out the VP in front of his peers directly, I asked the other managers for suggestions for changing his work process, so that they could work from home from time to time.

The supervisor of six receptionists who worked from home occasionally chimed in. She shared how she'd been able to automate document processing using a system they already had in house. It wouldn't cost him any additional money. I heard them on break arranging a meeting for her to show him how to redesign his process and enable the two clerks to work remotely.

Sometimes we're too close to the processes ourselves to see other ways to redesign them. Reach out to others in your organization to share process changes and get a fresh set of eyes to solve your work process challenges.

Lack of Technology Doesn't Have to Limit Innovation

You may feel constrained by the pace of technology adoption in your organization. Some companies are still questioning the value of instant messaging or enterprise social networking while others think those technologies are already outdated and are looking for what's next.

Wherever your organization stands, don't let technology limitations stand in your way. You can build simple project plans in Excel, create wikis in shared Word documents, and team member profiles in PowerPoint. Get creative!

If you haven't tried out some of the newer technologies in your organization and aren't sure how to set them up, find peers that do. There are early adopters in your organization who, through trial and error, figured it out and would be happy to share their knowledge.

But knowing how to set up and run a video conference is not the same as really understanding all of the creative ways teams can get more done and have more fun by optimizing technology. Try out new technology in the safety of your teams before venturing out to use it in higher visibility situations with senior leaders or customers. Trade best practices with your peers (and friends), watch videos on the internet, try ideas that you read in this book.

The more you try new things and model them for others, the more comfortable you'll get developing even more innovative ways to redesign your work processes.

Technology that can help you replace onsite work processes:

Shared calendars	Version control
CRM systems	Virtual whiteboards
VOIP phones	Wikis
VPN lines	Voicemail to email services
Remote access	Intranet sites
Electronic signature services	Virtual work groups
File sharing	Social networking software

What processes need to be redesigned to make your team more efficient in all of the ways you'll be working in the future? Consider that your team may have multiple ways of working all at the same time, for example: hoteling, open floor plan, flexible work arrangements and work from home or a third place.

_____

_____

_____

_____

Name 3-5 examples of work processes that waste time or are of little value that you could eliminate?

_____

_____

_____

_____

Have you gone entirely paperless? That can make a big difference to improve mobility no matter how your team works. If not, how could you get started?

_____

_____

_____

What technology could you use to make files, documents, and knowledge more accessible to everyone?

_____

_____

_____

_____

Meetings

1. We publish a timed agenda 24 hours in advance of every meeting.
2. We start meetings on time, so leader has the technology ready to go before the meeting begins.
3. We always include dial-in instructions in meeting invitations.
4. We vary the location and technology used for our meetings, leader selects location being respectful of the needs of both remote and onsite team members.
5. We park any unrelated or in depth conversations to keep our meetings on track.
6. All meetings are 50 minutes long to give time for team members to start meetings on time.
7. We take notes during meetings and publish them in a shared folder for those who are absent to stay up-to-date.

Mass Mailings

1. Advise all parties 5 days in advance, so that they will be in the office
2. Block off time on the shared calendar
3. Order necessary supplies so they are in-house on day of mailing

Now complete the Work Process Redesign Chart on page 187 and make a corresponding notes in your Team Alignment Plan on page 183.

Tool #5: Communication

❝ As a team we laid out a plan of core available hours and open communication that would allow each team member to be at the office or home while still allowing execution of project objectives. **❞**

- Manager, professional services firm

Tool #5 Communication

Staying connected is one of the biggest concerns managers (and employees) have about working in new environments, especially dispersed teams. That's because it just feels more natural to talk in person, bump into each other on the way to the copier, and gather together in an impromptu meeting, if necessary. It's how we grew up; it's what we know.

Working remotely not only removes a lot of that convenience, it presents other challenges as well. Reading non-verbal cues, managing introverted vs. extroverted styles, transferring knowledge, and even sharing a joke becomes more difficult when you can't see the people you're communicating with.

Before learning some of the strategies other teams use, analyze the current state of your own team's communications.

Communication SWOT Analysis

Complete the SWOT analysis on the following page. Your strengths are the communication practices that you do well and want to keep as your team works in new ways. Identifying weaknesses can help you identify opportunities for improving communication to collaborate better, improve inclusiveness, leverage technology and generally improve your communication practices. Threats help you recognize the importance of changing the way you currently communicate. They can be identified as the bad things that may happen to the organization or your team if you don't seize the opportunities to improve the way you connect.

Communication SWOT Analysis

Strengths	Weaknesses
Opportunities	**Threats**

Take a look at your communication strengths quadrant. Are any of these practices in jeopardy as your team works more flexibly or moves to a new office environment?

_____

_____

_____

_____

Are any of your strengths based on being together in the same place? These may need to be reworked in your new environment.

_____

_____

_____

_____

Regarding opportunities, weaknesses and threats—many times teams use the fact that they're going to be working more flexibly to address some issues that they've struggled with in the past. What are the three things in these quadrants that you'd most like to focus on?

_____

_____

_____

_____

Communication Tips for Dispersed Teams

1. **Technology is your friend.** You may not think so now, but if you embrace it, experiment and figure out what fits the personalities and needs of your team, you can come really close to delivering an "in person" experience.

2. **All relationships take work and virtual ones are no different.** If you put effort into building connections with remote co-workers, your experience will be much better than if you don't bother to communicate.

3. **Communication has to be more deliberate and planned.** Impromptu run-ins on the way to the lunchroom may not be possible. Pay attention to the kinds of topics that get covered on the fly, so that you can schedule meetings to cover those topics more deliberately, no matter where you work.

4. **Get personal.** Since you can't read cues, you're going to have to ask about feelings, tone, capacity, intention, agreement, understanding, etc. It may feel awkward at first, but it'll become second nature. Ask questions such as, "Does that make sense? Will that work for you? And, what do you think about that?"

5. **Virtual relationships are improved by spending time together in person.** Make the effort (and go to the expense) of getting team members together periodically. You'll reap the benefits of that experience for months to come.

6. **Vary communication styles for the benefit of both introverts and extroverts.** Technologies like the phone and web conferencing favor extroverts, while email and group chat may be preferred by introverts. Level the playing field by varying the ways you meet: web conference one week, group chat the next.

7. **You can read non-verbals even without seeing.** Emoticons, exclamation marks and length of communication all convey mood in the same way that a shoulder shrug, raised eyebrows and body posture can. Learn the communication styles of each of your team members and watch for

variances. When in doubt, ask them to share their reaction verbally.

8. **Knowledge sharing is still possible.** Determine what information needs to be shared, how frequently and with whom. Knowledge sharing can be made easier through collaboration software, wikis, and planned onsite visits. Decide what knowledge needs to be shared in person or via technology. Set dates on your schedules to make it happen.

9. **Plan for emergencies.** You may work for a manager who manages by walking around or have clients who want to reach you on the first ring. Remote employees can still be reachable and responsive even if they're not onsite. Reach agreement on the one form of technology you'll use to reach each other in an emergency. That way, everyone will actively monitor that one phone number or piece of equipment throughout the day.

10. **Have eyes and ears on the ground.** Encourage onsite team members to buddy up with someone offsite to keep them abreast of both business and personal news. Knowing what's going on will prevent offsite team members from feeling disconnected.

More Communication Tips for Dispersed Teams

- Set guidelines for how and when to communicate.

- Be open and honest.

- Greet every team member every day via IM, email or phone.

- Schedule a regular 1:1 meeting and stick to it. Don't reschedule.

- Instead of 1:1 meetings with each of your team members, create office hours during which your team can schedule time with you.

- Cultivate diversity of opinion.

- Clarify your intentions and expectations around why you work, when you work and when you expect team members to respond. Your pattern of answering emails between 10:00 and midnight may have your team members checking their phones, anxious to respond because they think that you're expecting it. Explain your expectations about their availability after hours.

- Record meetings or publish meeting notes in a shared file for team members who miss.

- Publish all team members' contact info in an easily retrievable place.

- Pay close attention to written communication. Look for emoticons, changes in tone or length of communication.

- Invite team members to create a personality profile and include their preferred communication styles. Customize your communication style to fit each employee.

Which of these tips would you like to try with your team?

_____

_____

Why?

_____

_____

_____

Did this list prompt any other ideas to improve communication with dispersed team members?

_____

_____

_____

_____

_____

_____

Reading Non-Verbals

What do you mean you can't read non-verbals from afar? We frequently hear this as a major concern, but it's easier than you think.

Consider this:

You know if someone is happy when you talk on the phone from the energy, pace and tone of their voice.

You can tell if someone is upset or crying by pauses in conversation, requesting that you call them back later, voice quivers or sniffling.

You might sense someone is busy if they send shorter than normal IMs or emails, their voice is brisk on the phone, they dispense with etiquette like asking "How was your weekend?" or don't use a greeting or sign their emails.

Distraction can be detected through keyboarding sounds, delays in responding, and asking if you can repeat the question.

The key is to look for changes to the person's natural communication style, and then deliberately inquire as to their mood after you've picked up on variances. Like, "I noticed it was taking you longer than normal to answer my IMs today. Are you really busy? Or Is everything okay?" Asking about the change (or making a presumption they can confirm or deny), gives you both an opportunity to read each other's non-verbals and clear the air.

Best to address it as it happens, so that your concerns or assumptions don't build over time.

Communication Challenges in Open Plan Work Environments

When the proportion of "me" to "we" space shifts, and "we" spaces are available in more configurations, you and your team face a whole new set of communication challenges.

Here are some issue areas to review with your team:

- Beware of the potential for over-monitoring. Since it's easier to see team members, how will you avoid jumping to conclusions about where they are and what they're doing? You don't want team members to feel like they have to rationalize every disappearance.

- Understand each other's tolerance for distractions, interruptions, noise and drop-ins. Knowing this in advance will help everyone be more productive.

- Think about how you will communicate your need for uninterrupted time when your team is chatty and prone to dropping by. One team uses table tents with a red side and a green side to indicate when they are doing focused work and when they are open to interruptions.

- Recognize that team members have different work styles and that one person's work style can derail another's productivity. An introvert in a sea of extroverts may struggle and need to negotiate dedicated quiet time or more time working alone, elsewhere in the building.

- Encourage everyone to identify their preferred work styles in advance of a move to a new work environment. Just because you can more easily drop in or work together in a space doesn't mean everyone will want to.

- You may still have team members working globally or remotely. How will you vary or blend onsite collaboration with technology?

What else do you anticipate being a challenge?

_____

_____

_____

_____

When Whiteboards Double as Doors

An IT manager expressed concern over his company's move to a brand new building with an open floor plan. It wasn't just himself he was worried about. He explained that even in their current cubicle setup, employees were repurposing moveable whiteboards to create doors for their workspaces.

He wondered how his team would manage the lack of privacy and anticipated noise levels in the new environment, if they couldn't even handle it in their current cube farm. He raised his concerns to leaders a couple of levels higher and was told that he'd just have to get used to it. Then he asked me for advice.

My counsel: Prepare for your move now by engaging your team members in conversations about work style preferences regarding collaboration and individual work. Based on the feedback, begin to form strategies together as to how you will honor each other's needs for privacy, quiet and thinking time in "me" spaces and the processes everyone will agree on for using the "we" spaces.

Identifying a plan will help you adjust to your new floor plan and give you a common language to work out conflicts.

Negotiating Hoteling Environments

Individual work style preferences, boundary control and the use of the workspaces themselves are areas for potential conflict in a hoteling environment.

Get together in advance to reach agreement on the set of "rules" you'll abide by to make hoteling work for your team. Agree on how you'll handle situations in which co-workers don't follow "team rules."

Etiquette matters in hoteling spaces where team members are sharing equipment, desks, chairs, etc. Simple things like not eating at your work space, abiding by the restrictions of private (and loud) spaces, and not reserving the same workspace day after day can be real sticking points.

Set up regular touch-base meetings as a team to discuss how it's going and modifications that need to be made to work practices, technology and workspaces.

Do you have hoteling "rules" that you should reference in your Team Alignment Plan?

_____

_____

_____

What other issues would you anticipate needing to address?

_____

_____

_____

Improve Communication By Respecting Work Styles

Another way to help your team improve trust and communicate more effectively is to understand each team member's work styles and preferences. This will help you in your individual interactions and provide perspective on how well-aligned your natural style is to that of your team members.

10 Questions to Ask Your Team Members:

1. What time of day are you most productive?

2. Do you like getting feedback? Do you prefer it be delivered verbally or in writing? Publicly or privately?

3. What characteristics do you value most in a leader?

4. Would you describe yourself as an introvert, extrovert or somewhere in between?

5. What is your preferred technology for communicating? (IM, phone, email, video, in person, etc.)

6. What are the top three behaviors that co-workers or your manager can do to build your trust and three that can erode it?

7. What limitations do you have in your schedule during the day/month/year that we need to work around?

8. How do you like to be rewarded? (gifts, letters of encouragement, more responsibility, lunch, etc.)

9. How disruptive are interruptions throughout your workday? Is it easy for you to get back to work right away, or does it cost you time and productivity? How would you prefer to handle them?

10. Are you a work-life integrator, separator or somewhere in the middle? (See box below.)

WorkLife Indicator

Dr. Ellen Kossek, researcher and author of *CEO of Me*, identified six work-life patterns that people fit into. Her WorkLife Indicator helps individuals and teams assess the approach each takes to managing the boundaries between work and family.

For example, two of those "flexstyles" include:

Integrators who fully integrate work and life

Separators who draw solid boundaries between the two

Understanding your own flexstyle and that of your team members provides a common understanding of the choices each makes and reduces assumptions about the reasons behind those behaviors. For more information, visit www.ccl.org or http://ellenkossek.lir.msu.edu/.

Feedback Preferences

In our workshops, when we ask managers to tell us whether they like feedback, most say "yes." But there are usually two or three managers who say they don't and another five or so that have mixed feelings about it. When the managers who like feedback hear the reasons that others don't, they're often surprised.

Some of the reasons they give for not liking feedback:

- It feels fake
- It feels too personal even if it's not meant to be
- I don't want to get feedback from someone I don't trust
- I don't want to receive feedback in public
- I think I do a good enough job and don't want to hear criticism

Learn the feedback preferences of your team members, so that giving and receiving feedback goes smoothly, especially on dispersed teams.

COMMUNICATION TECHNOLOGY

Are you fully utilizing technology that may be available to help you build a strong team and improve communication?

Remote access

Instant messaging

Group chat

CRM

Shared calendar & contacts

Micro-blogging

Enterprise social networking

Group meetings

Project management tools

Collaboration software

File sharing/public folders

Tele/video-conferencing

Virtual whiteboard

Wikis

Email

Which tech tools do you currently use? Which do you like and dislike?

_____

_____

_____

Do you know your team members preferences?

_____

_____

Are you varying the technology you use to suit the situation, or only relying on the ones you know?

_____

_____

Which ones would you like to try using with your team?

_____

_____

Who could be a great "tech ambassador" to show you how they use a piece of technology creatively to improve communication with your team?

_____

_____

How could you adjust meeting times, technology, and types of interaction to better fit with the rest of your team?

_____

_____

_____

Blame it on IT

Everyone loves to blame the IT department. They don't offer the right technology, it's too slow, it's not up-to-date. But IT has their own perspective.

They introduce technology and don't see people using it correctly, if at all. People don't come to them often enough, read their communications, or see how much they want to help.

When we have both IT people and people from the lines of business in the same workshop, it's funny. They get to hear both sides of the "argument."

And they realize that neither is the bad guy. IT wants to help, and most everyone else wants to learn. It's a matter of seeking each other out in an organization to work together to improve the technology you do have, and provide/listen to feedback about what needs to change.

Where we see the breakdown is in the creative uses of technology. By and large, IT serves up a tech buffet and provides instructions and support for using it. But who is sharing how the available technology can be used to solve business challenges?

Look into the tools you already have. For example, you might use the polling feature in a web conference to ask a fun, social question at the beginning of a meeting. Some teams are using IM systems instead of web conference software to share presentations. Others encourage meeting attendees to type their feedback into the chat feature of a web conference while others are talking, so they capture everyone's ideas.

Engage IT and engage each other, across departments and teams, to model best practices and share the best ways to use technology to optimize communication.

1. When we are working:

    a. We'll be accessible to clients and Firm employees by phone during the normal business hours of 8:30 a.m. CST through 5:30 p.m. CST.

    b. We'll sign onto Lync to communicate with team members throughout the day.

    c. We'll communicate by email to the entire team, where necessary, and at least the manager if we will not be available in the office by 9:30 a.m. (i.e. are running late or have a prior commitment preventing accessibility before this time).

    d. We'll respond to internal emails and voicemails from team members or manager within 1.5 hours.

    e. If a task is assigned by manager via email for a client need, we will acknowledge receipt and progress of task within 30 minutes of receipt.

    f. We'll respond to client emails and voicemails within 6 hours of receipt and no later than 24 hours, if absolutely necessary.

2. We will set Out-of-Office assistant in Outlook when we will not be accessible to clients during normal business hours of 8:30 a.m. CST through 5:30 p.m. CST.

3. We will update our calendars to establish days we are unavailable or out-of-office at a client site.

4. We currently display team contact information on a printed sheet to keep handy at our workspace. We'll make the same information available to our mobile workspace.

5. We will make a point to greet each other via Lync or in person to say good morning, socialize briefly and talk about pressing issues.

6. We will work to communicate with each other about training opportunities that we could benefit from as a team to promote combined education and discussion.

7. Our team will incorporate a new approach to calling quick "flash" meetings with all team members to address personal or professional topics relevant to the team. These can be initiated by any individual on the team and can be done by Lync conference, calendar request, or in-person round-up. Of course, this should consider the availability of all team members. This would not only provide a quick break from the norm, but also promote leadership experience in heading up a discussion, as well as knowledge sharing and open forum around pertinent topics.

8. We'll rely on the following technology for communicating:

   a. Remote Access

   b. Instant Messaging/Group Chats

   c. Project Tracking/Management - Identify a team standard project management, tracking, and collaboration tool to begin developing and using on all projects.

   d. Standard Templates - Focus on developing a standard template for our project databases and reports.

Turn to page 185 to write down notes from this section that you would like to include in your Team Alignment Plan.

SAMPLE: COMMUNICATION

Tool #6:
Team Building

" By getting the team together to work on the blueprint, it opened lines of communication between members. It caused everyone to think about how we communicate and reminded us to stop every so often and plan a fun team activity out of the office to improve moral and work-ing relationships. "

-Manager, professional services firm

Tool #6: Team Building

Team building? Did you say team building? Who has time for that?

If that's your response to this section, you're not alone. With the difficult recession and efforts to squeeze additional productivity out of the workforce (without adding headcount), team building efforts have, in large part, gone the way of the wagon wheel.

Who has time (or budget) for ropes courses, holiday parties or any other Friday afternoon activity away from the office?

Then add the complexity of building connection with team members living all over the globe, or those working flexible schedules, and it can feel downright hopeless.

But surveys show that employees want to feel connected, to work for the good of the team and to fulfill the mission of your organization. Engaged team members work harder and deliver higher levels of quality than those who are disengaged.

So how can you build connection and support relationship-building given these challenges?

#1 Consider the idea of "team building moments."

Rather than setting aside large chunks of time to connect and interact, set aside moments, literally minutes, at the beginning of a meeting, or in a virtual trivia game. Look for opportunities to make a brief, but meaningful connections with team members throughout the day, and as part of your work process. The ideas can be creative, silly, serious, and even related to the business you conduct.

#2 *Agree on expectations about participation.*

Some things might be served up as invitations for team members to participate, others you might consider mandatory. Be clear if you expect everyone to participate or not to avoid misunderstandings. It's also important to remind everyone that building connections is an expectation of the job, not an afterthought or for those who have time.

Here are some ways teams are staying connected:

1. Meet every morning on group IM chat to say good morning, socialize and talk about any pressing issues for the day.

2. Conduct virtual coffees/happy hours/birthday parties where no work discussion is allowed.

3. Ask team members to create a profile where they can post their contact information, work style preferences and things like hobbies, family information and photos (see sample).

4. Encourage team members to express their preferences regarding communication, feedback, recognition and schedule limitations, especially in their profile.

5. Interact with team members through professional social networking such as private LinkedIn groups or Yammer pages.

6. Assign an onsite "buddy" for team members who are frequently out of the office to keep them up on the latest gossip, happenings, etc.

7. Celebrate successes, recognize great work, and communicate with all team members electronically so everyone is kept in the loop.

8. Take 15-minute water cooler breaks during the day via technology, like group chat or video conferencing.

9. Try asking ice breaking questions at the start of every meeting.

10. Shared learning in the form of classes, book discussions and virtual conferences is a great way for team members to connect.

11. Rotate meeting leaders to enable team members to lead weekly conference calls, plan a monthly team building activity or organize an event.

12. To even the playing field, conduct team meetings while everyone onsite remains in their workstation.

13. Maintain a comprehensive calendar that includes team members' personal and professional obligations all in one space.

14. Plan quarterly retreats devoted to team building and getting to know each other.

15. Poll your team on work preferences or personal activities using virtual meeting software and share the results with the group.

16. Send remote employees care packages of products or promotional items that are available at headquarters.

17. Focus on one team member's profile every month and ask them to share about themselves.

18. Make a point to call remote workers on a regular basis to talk about personal matters.

19. Celebrate fifth Fridays with team building exercises or contests.

20. Store important documents on a shared drive that is accessible and used by everyone.

21. If your team is global, come in early or stay late one day a week to allow for phone meetings.

22. Use audio/visual technology to communicate in lieu of strictly using email. Leave a voicemail or record a brief video for updates.

Remember team building moments should be tailored to the personality of your team. If you like to have fun, then choose some of the wackier ideas on this list. If you tend to be a more serious group, then select a couple of activities you think might be enjoyable for your team.

Sample: Team Member Profile

[NAME]: Executive Assistant Office Phone: Mobile Phone: Email Address: Birthday: Work Anniversary:	**Best Way to Contact Me:** Email, IM, text. I prefer phone calls to be scheduled as juggling 2 positions without any structure can be tough. Work Schedule:

We are Chicago transplants, having moved here from Ohio about 8 years ago. My husband and I took our first trip to Chicago together when we were dating and fell in love with the city. When he got the opportunity to work here, we jumped at the chance to move! My husband refuses to hire anyone, so we are major do-it-youselfers! I have two children - a 14 year old daughter and a 12 year old son. I have been married for 16 years.

Work: In addition to working for Company A, I am also a graphic designer for an outdoor marketing company. We design and produce outdoor flags, banners, and the large advertising balloons. It can be interesting at times, but also a lot to juggle! I manage one major client and am also in charge of all their permit applications and managing their website.

Hobbies: I love to scrapbook and craft in general. I make my own wreaths, have made money on the side making hair bows & tutus, bake & decorate all my own cakes, take on lots of sewing projects and generally just enjoy being creative and making things with my own hands.

Birthday Celebrations: Not a big fan of celebrating my birthday. A brief acknowledgement or card is okay, but not big on a party, lunch or food brought in.

Most Productive: I am a night owl, but find it more difficult to work at night during the school year. I am sure in the summer when we can sleep in a little later, I will work into the wee hours!

Personality: In a business arena, I tend to be more introverted, but in my personal life, I am an extrovert for sure.

Preferred Recognition: Any recognition is good! It's always nice to hear that the work is appreciated.

Feedback Style: I like feedback, especially

Weakness: When I get overwhelmed, I tend to freeze. When I feel there is too much to do, I get stuck and don't know where to begin.

Favorites: Pizza, chocolate, Panera, tulips, pop music

10 Team Building Ideas for Introverts

These ideas above might sound good if you're working with a group of extroverted folks. But most of us work in mixed groups of introverts and extroverts. Consider engaging your team in a variety of activities that will appeal to different personalities and work styles. The introverts on your team will thank you.

1. Avoid impromptu discussions and activities. Introverts prefer structure and advance notice of discussion topics.

2. Schedule strategy sessions in advance to allow introverts time to research and think through ideas.

3. To make introverts feel more comfortable during introductions, ask participants to share work-related information in a short 30-second timeframe.

4. Focus ice-breaker activities on less personal information, such as their workspace or unusual jobs they've held.

5. Use personality assessments to help everyone understand each other's work styles.

6. Give new team members a little time to acclimate before jumping into team building activities.

7. Plan group outings at a ball game or other activity that makes conversation secondary.

8. Vary communication styles, such as teleconference vs. video conferencing, to accommodate the comfort level of your team.

9. If you are looking for feedback, group chat, wikis or blogs give introverts a safe and less pressured place to give comments after a meeting or team building activity.

10. Build team building moments that rely less on video, phone or meetings, and more on trading information via chat, email or shared drives.

Now that you've read through a range of team building practices, pick some things that you'd like your team to consider implementing:

_____

_____

_____

_____

Why do you think these practices, in particular, are well-suited to your team?

_____

_____

_____

Who on your team would be willing to lead these initiatives?

_____

_____

Add these to the draft of your Team Alignment Plan now on page 185.

Culture Map

Remote team members (or even those on flexible schedules) may miss out on some of the team experiences that help define your culture.

A Culture Map can help you identify onsite team activities and think about how to translate those activities so that all team members feel included, no matter when or where they work.

Cultural activities that may need to be redesigned:

Rewards

Thank you's and recognitions

Motivational activities

Disciplinary actions

Celebrations

News dissemination

To use the culture map, first consider all of the ways your team interacts. You'll find some examples in the list above, but feel free to add your own.

First Step: List a cultural activity on the top line.

Second Step: Identify your current practices in Column 1 and the impact on your team in Column 2.

Third Step: Identify ways to do it differently in Column 3. This is the place to brainstorm ways to translate your current practices to be more inclusive of all of your team members, no matter where or when they're working.

Here's an example of how to use the culture map to rethink how your team celebrates birthdays to help everyone, no matter where they work feel included.

Activity: Celebrating birthdays

Current Practices	Impact on Team	New Practices
Announce at monthly team meeting	Acknowledgement	Same
Bagel birthday breakfast 2nd Tuesday of each month	Socializing	Send gift card to remote employees. Do a video chat/conference to celebrate with remote employees. Record a happy birthday video for everyone.

This is a perfect activity to delegate to those fun-minded individuals on your team. Get as creative as you want to, but consider which activities will best fit the tone and culture of your team.

Birthdays Matter

At one non-profit organization, where leadership prided itself on their family-like culture, a little family dynamic was playing out under everyone's noses.

One of the women in the office made a special birthday casserole, but only for the people she liked most on her team. Everyone knew who her favorites were, and those who were not on her list wished they could be. That casserole smelled delicious.

When asked to name what they'd miss most when the team transitioned to new work from home schedules, one of this gal's favorite co-workers said "My birthday casserole." Meanwhile others on the team were pleased she'd no longer be able to play favorites.

The casserole discussion helped the team address an issue that had been brewing for a while, and it helped them think through new, enjoyable, and more inclusive ways to celebrate birthdays going forward.

If you think it's a just a birthday celebration. Think again. Birthdays matter... a lot.

How much of your culture is based on being onsite? What activities specifically?

_____

_____

_____

_____

_____

Who could you ask to help you generate ideas for translating some of those practices for team members who flex their hours or work remotely?

_____

_____

What team building moments would you like to implement with your team?

_____

_____

_____

_____

_____

A Tale of Two Companies

Every year in December, my team had the same conversation. We all work virtually and felt compelled to celebrate Christmas (in our case) together.

Or so we thought.

I'd bring it up in our weekly team meetings for weeks, but we could never decide on what to do. Christmas would get closer and we'd casually acknowledge that we'd never gotten around to celebrating.

Until one year, I suggested that we should just acknowledge that while it seemed like a nice idea, none of us really felt the need to do it. It didn't really fit with the personality of our team. So we all agreed not to celebrate—no harm, no foul—and moved on.

Compare that to a recent set of complaints I heard from satellite offices of a large corporation. Every year the company hosts a Thanksgiving celebration at the HQ office, but doesn't offer similar celebrations in their satellite locations. News of the HQ celebration travelled by word-of-mouth but was never actually acknowledged by senior leadership. Employees from those satellite offices told us about how left out they felt that no one had bothered to devise a parallel celebration for the rest of their employees and what a difference it would make to their goal of creating a "one company" mindset.

How simple it would be for the company to arrange catering for all of their satellite offices and to host a video conference of the CEO wishing everyone a happy holiday from HQ? Fairly easy.

Team Building

1. Acknowledgments - During our monthly team meeting, each team member will have the opportunity to share two acknowledgements for the previous month, one for themselves and one for someone else.

2. We will continue to schedule lunches or events to celebrate accomplishments or give thanks to team members.

3. Our manager will host a team event twice a year for team members and family.

4. We will continue to celebrate birthdays and other special events by planning ahead to accommodate remote working or unavailable team members.

5. Twice a month, we will schedule to bring our lunch (or order in) and play a game of the team's choice over the lunch break.

6. Acknowledgements - During our monthly team meeting, each team member will have the opportunity to share two acknowledgements.

Add your team building ideas to your Team Alignment Plan draft now on page 185.

Keeping It Real

" The Team Alignment Plan…was helpful, and I especially liked the fact that my manager allowed her direct reports the opportunity to review and provide feedback. "

- Employee, biotech firm

Keeping It Real

Throughout this book we've encouraged you to consider what the future of work looks like for your team. We've also encouraged you to learn new tools, best practices and approaches, and customize them for the function, culture and work styles of your team.

The Team Alignment Plan is a tool you can use with your team to document and discuss these new approaches to work. Hopefully you've made some notes as you worked your way through this book. Drafting and finalizing it is the final step in the process.

Managers tend to favor one of two approaches:

1. Draft the plan, share it with your team to get feedback and make revisions, and then finalize the plan with your team.

2. Discuss the idea of building a plan with your team. Then encourage team members to draft sections. Once you see what they've drafted, you finalize the plan and share it with your team. You can build in additional feedback and draft reviews with them, if you like.

Agree with your team on how you'll keep the plan alive--decide how frequently you'll review it and in what forum. Also, determine who will be responsible for holding the team accountable for doing so?

Tips for Building Your Team Alignment Plan

- **Not everything you put in your plan has to be new.** Some teams cut and paste their values into it, for example, from previous work they've done. Or if you have team building activities you've done for years, you might not need to determine new activities, just document your current practices.

- **Your plan doesn't have to be exhaustive.** We've covered a lot of information in this book, now it's up to you and your team to determine the kinds of activities you all might benefit from.

- **Remember to be specific.** It won't help to say in your plan, "Determine how we'll hold each other accountable." If you recognize the need to do it, then do it now. Decide together how you'll do that, and put the specific practices down in your plan.

- **Use your Team Alignment Plan as an onboarding tool.** Other managers have told us that their plan saves them time when onboarding new team members. Rather than guessing about how the team operates, your new team member can clearly see what is expected.

- **Consider it from a new employee's point-of-view.** Read through it and ask yourself, "If I were new to this team, would I understand how the team operates? Would it help me hit the ground running?" If the answer is no, then clarify and be more specific about some of the things you've included in your plan.

- **See employee input.** This is a team effort from which everyone will benefit. Besides, many hands make light work. You might be surprised by the great ideas that come from their participation.

- **Make this plan an organic document.** Review it regularly so it stays current and continues to address your team's changing needs.

What approach will you use to draft and finalize your Team Alignment Plan?

_____

_____

_____

_____

How will you keep it updated?

_____

_____

_____

_____

Who will be responsible for speaking up if the team strays from the plan or goes back to its old ways?

_____

_____

_____

_____

1. In preparation of the monthly team meeting occurring in the last month of each quarter, the team will be prompted via a calendar appointment to review the Team Alignment Plan and note any necessary changes or updates. These will be discussed as a group during the meeting.

2. The plan will be adjusted as policies, procedures or standardized approaches are developed that impact the way our team collaborates, communicates or completes our work.

Add ideas to your Team Alignment Plan draft on page 186.

Final Considerations

At this point, you might be thinking, "I don't have time for this." We all have too much work and not enough time to manage the work we have on our plate. Most of us know that there's a better way to do our work, but we don't have time to change.

Managers who devote time to the process have reaped the benefits. In the National Workplace Flexibility Study which tested the Team Alignment Plan[1] approach, managers were asked how they felt about workplace flexibility after participating in the study. They responded that they felt more comfortable with managing flexibility, felt their team had improved in key areas, and believed that even productivity and customer service improved.

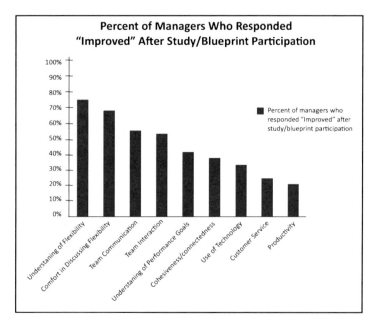

For more information about the study and to hear managers talk about their experiences, visit www.workplaceflex.org.

---

1 The Team Alignment Plan was referred to as a Flex Team Blueprint in the study.

One manager from the study put it this way:

> **"** I have to admit, before I participated I did feel like the investment of time wasn't worth it for my team. I had an established team, we had been around quite a bit, we were a well-functioning team and I frankly questioned the value of my time investment. (After going through the study process) I felt having a Team Alignment Plan memorialized our values and unwritten expectations. We function better as a team. We crystallized our meaning for being here and established our values. **"**

If you decide to jump in with both feet and make time for this process, I applaud you and support your efforts. I hope this book will be a launching point for a bigger conversation with your team. It's a conversation employees desire.

Only 47% of people surveyed said their employers regularly seek input from employees and only 37% said their organization makes changes based on that feedback. - American Psychological Association's Center for Organizational Excellence, March 5, 2013.

You may decide not to make the time to go through the process and formalize your Team Alignment Plan. But, if you take even a single idea and implement it, you and your team will be better for it.

The best practices in this book come from managers' real life experiences. But these ideas are just the tip of the iceberg. There are so many more out there, and the best learning comes from sharing ideas with others. Talk with your peers about how they're navigating non-traditional work environments. Then visit us at www.lifemeetswork.com for additional tips and story sharing around the Team Alignment Plan process.

Templates

Team Alignment Plan

Navigating Change

We've developed this set of principles that everyone on our team agrees to follow, so that we can improve team mobility while maintaining our strong company culture.

Team Goal

Our professional commitment as a team is to our clients and delivering high quality engagement results, while adhering to our company's policies and procedures. Our goal is to accomplish this high level of client service by juggling our professional responsibilities with our personal needs throughout each day, week, or month.

The goal of this agreement is to identify the values and actions that each of us should exhibit as a member of this team.

Team Metrics

We're going to measure our effectiveness as a team through these metrics:
1. Higher productivity
2. Better engagement
3. Faster response time
4. Greater project knowledge
5. Increased confidence and comfort in leading meetings

Performance

These are our "rules of engagement" as a team in consideration of our flexible working environment.
1. We are committed to being experts in our field and invest time in reinforcing our subject matter expertise.

2. We will operate within the highest ethical standards when interacting with both internal and external clients, and the team.
3. We will escalate any client service failures immediately to our manager regardless of working status.
4. We will communicate and consider the Client's best interests in determining workplan strategies, timelines, and recommendations on projects.
5. We understand that delivering the most high-quality, thorough and accurate work product sometimes means long hours or extra commitment.
6. We will manage the client's expectations by asking questions regarding desired scope of work, timelines, communication, and availability. We will document and manage the client's requests in these areas to deliver as promised and exceed their expectations.
7. Under all conditions, we will:
   a. Commit to one team meeting per month to review project assignment, revenue, and hold an open discussion regarding team practices, improvements, and needs.
   b. Document engagement deadlines and communicate those deadlines appropriately via email notification, workplan, and calendar updates.
   c. Adhere to internal team policy of completing client project status reports and summary of savings documents by the 5th of each month.
   d. Perform no more than weekly updates to project tracking systems utilized for visibility by the team and supervisors for real-time communication of project status.
   e. Adhere to Firm deadlines regarding time entry, release, and approval; engagement revenue recognition; and project status updates.
   f. Share information, as permitted by our manager, which is obtained or developed during our engagements to other team members and Firm members to promote knowledge sharing across the organization.
   g. Request feedback and convey appreciation to our clients regarding our engagement progress, onsite fieldwork, and

results.

8. We will stay organized on our projects and strive to develop and communicate best practices for use by the team to deliver a standard high-quality work product.
9. We will adhere to Firm and team filing policies to ensure mail and electronically received communication is appropriately stored and visible to pertinent parties.
10. We will apply the utmost protection of client and Firm confidential documentation.
11. We will uphold our responsibility to be mindful of our team members' confidential information and personal conditions.

Here are the ways we agree to keep each other "in the loop" about progress toward our individual and collective goals:

1. One-on-One meetings - these can be live, virtual, or by phone as long as an agenda is prepared and project work plan updates are incorporated and discussed.
2. Project Tracking - this is the team preferred method for managing day-to-day activities, information capture and sharing, progress and needs.
3. Weekly Flash Report - Bullet point email that addresses goals for the week.
   a. Establishes tasks completed, obstacles, and next steps.
   b. This email should be addressed to Manager and copied to all team members to promote knowledge sharing.

Capacity/Resiliency

1. We will not "over-promise" and commit ourselves to unrealistic deadlines. We will request deadlines from internal and external clients and then negotiate delivery based on the resources we have available.
2. We maintain relationships with independent contractors so that we can ramp up and down as our workload fluctuates. Team members will help manage workload by asking for freelance help when their work expands beyond capacity.
3. Each team member will set an annual work-life goal. Team members

will review those goals with their manager as part of quarterly review meetings and will receive an incentive for meeting that goal.
4. As a team, we aim for at least 90% utilization of our PTO time each year. The team will be treated to a catered lunch and each member will receive a company apparel item of their choice when we hit that goal.

When & Where We Work

1. Staff can work a maximum of two days a week from home.
2. All team members are required to work in the office on Thursdays.
3. We will update our calendar to establish days we are working remotely to help meeting organizers who are relying on calendar information.
4. We strive to cover every team member's flexibility needs and expect the same coverage for ourselves in return.

Work Process

Meetings
1. We publish a timed agenda 24 hours in advance of every meeting.
2. We start meetings on time, so leader has the technology ready to go before the meeting begins.
3. We always include dial-in instructions in meeting invitations.
4. We vary the location and technology used for our meetings, leader selects location being respectful of the needs of both remote and onsite team members.
5. We park any unrelated or in depth conversations to keep our meetings on track.
6. All meetings are 50 minutes long to give time for team members to start meetings on time.
7. We take notes during meetings and publish them in a shared folder for those who are absent to stay up-to-date.

Mass Mailings
1. Advise all parties 5 days in advance, so that they will be in the office
2. Block off time on the shared calendar

3. Order necessary supplies so they are in-house on day of mailing

Communication

1. When we are working:
   a. We'll be accessible to clients and Firm employees by phone during the normal business hours of 8:30 a.m. CST through 5:30 p.m. CST.
   b. We'll sign onto Lync to communicate with team members throughout the day.
   c. We'll communicate by email to the entire team, where necessary, and at least the manager if we will not be available in the office by 9:30 a.m. (i.e. are running late or have a prior commitment preventing accessibility before this time).
   d. We'll respond to internal emails and voicemails from team members or manager within 1.5 hours.
   e. If a task is assigned by manager via email for a client need, we will acknowledge receipt and progress of task within 30 minutes of receipt.
   f. We'll respond to client emails and voicemails within 6 hours of receipt and no later than 24 hours, if absolutely necessary.
2. We will set Out-of-Office assistant in Outlook when we will not be accessible to clients during normal business hours of 8:30 a.m. CST through 5:30 p.m. CST.
3. We will update our calendars to establish days we are unavailable or out-of-office at a client site.
4. We currently display team contact information on a printed sheet to keep handy at our workspace. We'll make the same information available to our mobile workspace.
5. We will make a point to greet each other via Lync or in person to say good morning, socialize briefly and talk about pressing issues.
6. We will work to communicate with each other about training opportunities that we could benefit from as a team to promote combined education and discussion.
7. Our team will incorporate a new approach to calling quick "flash"

meetings with all team members to address personal or professional topics relevant to the team. These can be initiated by any individual on the team and can be done by Lync conference, calendar request, or in-person round-up. Of course, this should consider the availability of all team members. This would not only provide a quick break from the norm, but also promote leadership experience in heading up a discussion, as well as knowledge sharing and open forum around pertinent topics.

8. We'll rely on the following technology for communicating:
   a. Remote Access
   b. Instant Messaging/Group Chats
   c. Project Tracking/Management - Identify a team standard project management, tracking, and collaboration tool to begin developing and using on all projects.
   d. Standard Templates - Focus on developing a standard template for our project databases and reports.

Team Building

1. Acknowledgments - During our monthly team meeting, each team member will have the opportunity to share two acknowledgements for the previous month, one for themselves and one for someone else.
2. We will continue to schedule lunches or events to celebrate accomplishments or give thanks to team members.
3. Our manager will host a team event twice a year for team members and family.
4. We will continue to celebrate birthdays and other special events by planning ahead to accommodate remote working or unavailable team members.
5. Twice a month, we will schedule to bring our lunch (or order in) and play a game of the team's choice over the lunch break.
6. Acknowledgements - During our monthly team meeting, each team member will have the opportunity to share two acknowledgements.

Keeping It Real

1. In preparation of the monthly team meeting occurring in the last month of each quarter, the team will be prompted via a calendar appointment to review the Team Alignment Plan and note any necessary changes or updates. These will be discussed as a group during the meeting.
2. The plan will be adjusted as policies, procedures or standardized approaches are developed that impact the way our team collaborates, communicates or completes our work.

Team Alignment Plan

Navigating Change

Here are the changes we're facing that prompt us to develop this plan...

Team Goal

We are on a mission to achieve the following goal(s) as a team...

Team Metrics

We're going to measure our effectiveness as a team through these metrics...

DRAFT YOUR TEAM ALIGNMENT PLAN

Performance

These are the values and behaviors that each of us should exhibit as a member of this team...

Here are the ways we agree to hold ourselves and each other accountable for getting work done...

Capacity/Resiliency

We recognize the importance of being transparent about overwork and stress and commit to do the following things to mitigate it...

When & Where We Work

We've openly discussed the needs of our team members to work in ways that work best for them and our team. Here are our guidelines...

Work Process

Here are the new work processes we've designed to improve our team's effectiveness no matter where and when we're working...

Communication

We're going to try some new approaches (and new technology) to improve communication within our team...

Team Building

We've come up with some new strategies for building team-building moments into our daily activities...

Keeping it Real

We're committed to keeping this plan relevant by doing the following...

Work Process Redesign Chart

To use this chart, start by listing the work processes you want to redesign. Then, identify your current approach in Column 1, the negative impact on your team in Column 2, and ways to do it differently in Column 3.

Work Process: _____

Current	Impact	New

WORK PROCESS REDESIGN

WORK PROCESS REDESIGN

Work Process: _____

Current	Impact	New

Work Process: _____

Current	Impact	New

WORK PROCESS REDESIGN

Culture Map

This is the place to brainstorm ways to translate your current practices to be more inclusive of all of your team members, no matter where or when they're working.

To use the culture map, start by listing a cultural activity on the top line. Then, identify your current practices in Column 1 and the impact on your team in Column 2. Finally, identify ways to do it differently in Column 3.

Activity: _____

Current Practices	Impact on Team	New Practices

Activity: _____

Current Practices	Impact on Team	New Practices

CULTURE MAP

Flash Report

A flash report is a quick way for team members to check in with each other and enables you to see if a team member's activities and priorities are in line with your expectations. Are they getting things done? Are the things that they're working on the "right" things for the organization?

For the team, it creates transparency around the work getting done and puts everyone's mind at ease. If there are questions or concerns, it becomes the trigger for people to pick up the phone and iron things out.

Decide whether employees should share flash reports with everyone on the team or only with you.

What's in a flash report?

A flash report is a short email. It's designed to be easy to write and to read. Use short sentences or even bullet points to answer these three questions:

1. What are the three most important things you accomplished this week?

2. What are the three most important things you will accomplish next week?

3. Is there anything you need from your team members in order to accomplish these things?

Jaime's Flash Report
Week ending 2/17

Accomplished:
- Marketing copy written for sell sheet and circulated for review
- Continued website update plans and sent inquiries to three vendors
- Press kit updated and sent to designer

Next Week:
- Get newsletter drafted and ready for review
- Draft press release, blog posts, and social media plan for book launch
- Review "Client A's" toolkit notes and make edits

I Need:
- I need your sell sheet comments back by end of business on Monday. *Important deadline! Our designer is on vacation after Thursday.*
- Plan to receive newsletter draft on Wednesday and return notes by EOB Friday

SAMPLE FLASH REPORT

Acknowledgments

No (wo)man is an island and that is certainly true in my case. My sincere thanks to Jaime Leick, my editor, and Jenn Prusak, my assistant, who worked tirelessly to get this book over the finish line. Without their insights and inspiration, it would have a boring title, lack visual interest, and have far too many words to be interesting. Thanks for your commitment to the success of Life Meets Work and for your friendship.

To Teresa Hopke, who took a leap of faith to join me on this incredible journey to change the quality of life for people in organizations everywhere. Thank you for your wisdom and challenging me to take risks.

My tremendous gratitude for Jennifer Fraone, Kathy Kacher, Delta Emerson, Kathy Weaver, Linda Brennan, Susan Nester, Lucy Kender and the hundreds of managers we trained as part of the National Workplace Flexibility Study. This study was a labor of love for Jennifer, Kathy and me as we forged a new approach for managers and a deeper bond with each other.

Most importantly, thank you to my family. Joe, Nate, Sean and Tom were patient and loving while I traveled extensively, training even more managers to test out the process in this book. Their undying belief in me and the work I do is a precious gift that I treasure every day.

For all of our clients—past, present and future—and to all of the people who work in those organizations, thank you for sharing your experiences, and for being honest and open about the impact of the changing workplace on your personal and professional lives. Ultimately, it is for you that I do this work.

Lastly, to my mom, Eileen Thompson, who broke the glass ceiling for me and for many women during her long career. Thank you for being such a strong role model and for teaching me that I could be or do anything in life, if I worked hard enough.

About the Author

As president of Life Meets Work, Kyra Cavanaugh helps leaders think differently about how work gets done. She works with organizations of all types to incorporate innovative workforce practices into their day-to-day operations through practical, business-based approaches to workplace flexibility, distributed teams and remote work.

Kyra developed the Team Alignment Plan after training hundreds of managers on how to lead teams working in dispersed, flexible, hoteling and open plan environments. This approach helps leaders incorporate new ways of working into their business processes, improving both business results and employee experience.

Kyra co-authored the ground-breaking National Workplace Flexibility Study and is an advisor to the Families and Work Institute/SHRM workflex partnership. She's a nationally-recognized speaker, blogger and commentator on workforce issues, and the recipient of the 2011 Work-Life Rising Star Award from Alliance for Work-Life Progress.

Before founding Life Meets Work in 2007, Kyra spent almost 20 years in the consumer packaged goods industry. Working in many functional areas for companies like Quaker Oats, Keebler, Dominick's Finer Foods, and Willard Bishop, she managed change and developed innovative approaches to solving business challenges.

www.lifemeetswork.com

Introducing the Team Alignment Plan Workshop

Based on the book Who Works Where [And Who Cares?]

by Kyra Cavanaugh

The Team Alignment Plan (TAP) workshop is a unique learning experience designed to help teams move toward greater collaboration and effectiveness. Teams engage in dynamic exercises and best practice sharing to progress in the six key areas discussed in this book: Performance, Capacity & Resiliency, When & Where We Work, Work Process, Communication, and Team Building. This powerful workshop was developed by Kyra Cavanaugh and her firm, Life Meets Work, to help leaders and their teams think differently about the way they work in order to improve the effectiveness of individuals and their teams.

The TAP training approach includes an in-person facilitated workshop, participant workbook, group coaching, individual coaching, and leadership assessment. A facilitator's guide and materials licensing option is available for organizations that want to plan and facilitate their own TAP workshops and scale training to a larger audience.

For more information, please contact kcavanaugh@lifemeetswork.com.

Notes

Notes

Notes

Notes